CW00349069

CHARLTON ATHLETIC
On This Day

CHARLTON ATHLETIC
On This Day

History, Facts & Figures
from Every Day of the Year

MATTHEW EASTLEY

CHARLTON ATHLETIC
On This Day

History, Facts & Figures from Every Day of the Year

All statistics, facts and figures are correct as of 1st August 2011

© Matt Eastley

Matt Eastley has asserted his rights in accordance with the Copyright, Designs and Patents Act 1988 to be identified as the author of this work.

Published By:
Pitch Publishing (Brighton) Ltd
A2 Yeoman Gate
Yeoman Way
Durrington
BN13 3QZ

Email: info@pitchpublishing.co.uk
Web: www.pitchpublishing.co.uk

First published 2011

A catalogue record for this book is available from the British Library.

ISBN: 978-1-9080510-9-7

Typesetting and origination by Pitch Publishing. Printed in Great Britain. Manufacturing managed by Jellyfish Print Solutions Ltd.

This book is dedicated to my grandfather, Jim Eastley (1909-1980), who first started following Charlton in the 1930s and introduced my father Derek and, in turn, myself and my older brother Gavin to this great club.

FOREWORD BY DEREK HALES

It is with genuine delight that I am writing the foreword to this new book by Matt Eastley entitled *Charlton Athletic On This Day*.

Most of my footballing days at Charlton meant so much to me. It played such an important part in my life that I can never forget it.

The Charlton fans have always been fantastic to me and I will remember them forever. My Charlton goalscoring record will probably never be beaten now because players move around so much more than they did but everyone is willing to have a go!

There have been plenty of great players that have pulled on the famous red shirt and many of them are featured in this book. As too, are all the important events that have shaped this great club, including great matches, like the 1998 play-off final, promotions, relegations and groundsharing.

There's also a reference to my altercation on the pitch with Mike Flanagan! That incident never played a big part in my footballing life but supporters always remember it.

I hope you enjoy the book. Good luck to you all.

ACKNOWLEDGEMENTS

I am indebted to the contributions of a number of people who have made the task of writing this book considerably easier. I am sure I speak for thousands of Charlton fans when I say that the first name that springs to mind when considering the club's history, statistics, facts and trivia is that of Colin Cameron. Colin has produced two volumes of work which are, quite simply, masterpieces. The brilliant *Valiant 500* and *Home and Away with Charlton Athletic 1920-2004* are both immense pieces of work containing invaluable material.

Colin was helpful and supportive from the word go and assisted me with some of the more difficult dates. He also very kindly read the manuscript and made some invaluable amendments, suggestions and clarifications.

I also drew heavily on Richard Redden's excellent history of Charlton Athletic, originally published in 1990 and then updated in 1993 to include the glorious return to The Valley in 1992.

Like Colin, Richard has also been very helpful, especially with his first class knowledge of Charlton in the very early years before they became a league club.

I must also thank Rick Everitt, the uber-fan who has secured his own place in Charlton's history. His pioneering efforts in leading the campaign to bring his beloved club back to The Valley, must never be forgotten. His *Battle for the Valley* is an superbly written, well-researched book which I am also indebted to. Thanks also to Charlton's Matt Wright for his help in the early stages of the project and to Derek Hales. I am honoured and thrilled that 'Killer' was kind enough to write the foreword this book.

Finally thanks to all my family and especially my wife Lisa and young daughter Alice for their tolerance, patience and understanding while I spent long, long hours on this labour of love.

INTRODUCTION

We all think our club is special. We can change our car or our job. Hell, we can even change our sex if we wish. But we can't change our football team. Through the good times and bad times, we're saddled with the damn outfit.

Once we've nailed our colours to the mast, nothing can sway us. A football team gets under your skin in a way that nothing else can. We love them and we hate them. But we can never leave them. And so it is with Charlton and I.

They've thrilled me, hurt me, made my day, and ruined my weekend. I took my time coming to them, especially as they were right under my nose. My local team and the club of choice of my dad, and his dad before him. It took me a while to understand the significance of those two factors. When I finally fell for them, I fell big.

At first it was all about Hales, Flanagan and Peacock. Then new names like Walsh and Lee, like Mortimer and Leaburn. Then fast forward to the days of Mendonca, Kinsella and Rufus and to modern-day heroes like Parker and Bent. And, like the old terrace song goes, if you know your history you start to appreciate the significance of greats like Seed, Leary, Welsh, Firmani and Bartram.

By any stretch of the imagination, Charlton's story is a remarkable one. The first club to rise from the old Division Three to the old Division One, eventually finishing runners-up, the team that staged the greatest-ever recovery in a league match, the first club to use a substitute, the first club to retain a place in Division One via the play-offs and the first club since the war to up-sticks and groundshare, only to return home in glory seven years later, and the team which won a famous play-off final still considered one of the finest games ever staged at Wembley.

Yes, we all think our club is special. I *know* that Charlton Athletic really is. Come On You Reds!

Matt Eastley

CHARLTON ATHLETIC
On This Day

JANUARY

FRIDAY 1st JANUARY 1988

With sore heads and bleary eyes, several hundred hardy Charlton fans rose early to make the long trip north for a league match against Manchester United. The Addicks fans were rewarded for their loyalty with one of the finest performances ever by a Charlton goalkeeper. Bob Bolder was simply outstanding, repelling wave after wave of attack from a United side which contained Bryan Robson, Gordon Strachan and Brian McClair. Manager Alex Ferguson said after the match: "It was one of the best displays of goalkeeping I have ever seen." The United fans were not happy – later, one rang a radio station to say that unless United could beat "joke outfits like Charlton Athletic" they would never win anything…

MONDAY 1st JANUARY 2001

A fine header from striker Jonatan Johansson gave Charlton their first win over Arsenal in 44 years. The Finnish international rose majestically to nod a Graham Stuart cross past Gunners keeper Alex Manninger after 39 minutes. With 15 minutes remaining, Arsenal were thrown a lifeline when Tomas Danilevicius was brought down in the area, but Addicks keeper Dean Kiely saved brilliantly from Nelson Vivas's penalty. It was a fine win for Charlton in front of 20,043 fans. "This is the most satisfying win since I arrived here in the summer," said Johannson after the game.

TUESDAY 1st JANUARY 2002

When Ipswich Town raced into a 2-0 lead after just five minutes at The Valley, Addicks fans could have been forgiven for thinking that the men in red had been less than abstemious the night before. Future Addick Marcus Bent scored both goals, the first after just 54 seconds. Stunned into action, Charlton suddenly remembered they were playing a Premiership match and set about repairing the damage. On 16 minutes, John Robinson fired a low drive past Matteo Sereni and then Scott Parker equalised just after the half hour. The comeback was complete when Jason Euell smashed home from close range on the hour mark. At the end of the 3-2 win, the Charlton fans directed a chant towards their friends from East Anglia which suggested that, though their team had been 2-0 up, they had failed to capitalise on their advantage. Or words to that effect…

SATURDAY 2nd JANUARY 1993

With a warm glow still radiating around the club after the glorious return to The Valley, Charlton travelled to Leeds United for a third-round FA Cup tie. At the time, Leeds were the reigning English champions, winning the old Football League Division One in its final season. After 70 minutes there was joyous mayhem on the away terraces as Garry Nelson fired a loose ball into the roof of the net in front of the stunned United followers to set up a potential cup upset. But it wasn't to be – while Addicks fans were still celebrating, Leeds surged forward and Gary Speed beat Bob Bolder to make it 1-1. United made short work of Charlton in the replay, winning 3-1 at The Valley.

MONDAY 3rd JANUARY 1983

Charlton boss Lennie Lawrence said his side looked like "world beaters" in the first half and "schoolboys" in the second as they managed to turn a 3-1 advantage against Sheffield Wednesday into a 5-4 loss. It was the first time in 15 years that nine goals had been scored in one game at Hillsborough. Charlton responded to an early Andy McCulloch goal with strikes from Martin Robinson, Steve White and Carl Harris. But The Owls, managed by Jack Charlton, stormed back and blitzed the Addicks with four goals in 15 minutes.

SATURDAY 3rd JANUARY 1987

Years before the 'she fell over' chant took root among football fans, there was a bizarre incident at Carrow Road involving Charlton left-back Mark Reid and referee David Axcell. Charlton led Norwich 1-0 thanks to a 22nd-minute goal from Mark Stuart. The Addicks looked like taking all three points back to London but, with 16 minutes to go, Canaries striker Wayne Biggins equalised with a goal that Charlton were adamant did not cross the line. In the ensuing protests, Reid pushed over Axcell, who suffered concussion and was taken to hospital. Though Axcell later confirmed that the incident was an accident, Reid was still charged with bringing the game into disrepute and found guilty of technical assault. Despite not being suspended or fined, Reid was reprimanded and warned as to his future conduct.

TUESDAY 4th JANUARY 2011

Following a 4-2 home defeat to Swindon Town, new Charlton chairman Michael Slater took swift action and announced the departure of manager Phil Parkinson, assistant manager Tim Breacker and first-team coach Mark Kinsella. Slater said: "Clearly improvement is needed on the field. The team has not won in the league since November and recent performances have simply not been good enough."

SATURDAY 5th JANUARY 1980

It's an awful long way to Wrexham and 'awful' was the apposite word for an Addicks horror show in north Wales. The 10,670 in the Racecourse Ground saw the home side inflict Charlton's biggest FA Cup defeat in terms of goal difference in this third-round tie. Charlton keeper Jeff Wood was beaten six times and, after the match, Addicks boss Mike Bailey issued a quote to the press which was interesting for its understated nature: "We'll have to tighten up in defence," he said.

SATURDAY 5th JANUARY 1985

Charlton boss Lennie Lawrence was his usual sardonic self after Mark Aizlewood scored at the third attempt as the Addicks drew at Tottenham Hotspur in the third round of the FA Cup. Spurs were leading 1-0 when referee Alan Gunn awarded Charlton a penalty in the 50th minute. Aizlewood's spot kick was saved by Clemence, who then parried away a follow-up from Steve Gritt. The ball then fell perfectly for Aizlewood, who slotted the ball home. Lawrence said: "We had that move worked out in training," and added, "it wasn't a bad penalty. I think Clemence moved."

SUNDAY 5th JANUARY 1986

At the start of the 1985/86 season there was no football on TV due to an ongoing row over broadcasting rights. When it was finally resolved, the first live match was the third-round tie between Charlton and West Ham United at Selhurst Park. Charlton played admirably but were undone two minutes from time when Tony Cottee scored from close range. Addicks manager Lennie Lawrence, though, was still a proud man: "We gave a good account of ourselves," he said. "My 11 players could not have done any more than they did." His opposite number John Lyall agreed, saying: "Charlton deserved a draw."

SATURDAY 6th JANUARY 1951

Though Swedish amateur Hans Jeppson only played 11 times for Charlton, he was nothing short of a sensation. Snapped up on this day by Jimmy Seed to play for the club while he was on business in London, Jeppson made his debut on January 13th against Sheffield Wednesday with Charlton in grave danger of relegation. He produced a series of brilliant performances, including a hat-trick against Arsenal and, in total, scored nine goals for the club to help save them from the drop. With film star good looks, he was adored by the fans who, following his final game on March 31st, presented him with a cup inscribed: "In appreciation of services and enjoyment given to supporters."

SATURDAY 6th JANUARY 1996

Daily Express reporter Kevin Moseley said Charlton's shock cup victory over Premiership side Sheffield Wednesday was a case of "a sleeping giant stirring". The Addicks played superbly and sent The Owls packing thanks to an early Kim Grant opener and a Paul Mortimer penalty. Moseley described the victory as "a declaration of intent" for future success. Boss Alan Curbishley claimed his side were invariably overlooked when the media talked about sides that were on the up: "They talk about Derby, Norwich and Birmingham, but always leave us out," he said.

SATURDAY 6th JANUARY 2001

Five days after beating Arsenal in SE7, Charlton faced non-league Dagenham and Redbridge at The Valley for an FA Cup third-round tie. The Essex side were surely easy lambs to the slaughter for an Addicks team on the crest of a wave. What actually happened was that, for 86 minutes, the Addicks fans squirmed with embarrassment as they were outplayed by Garry Hill's men. Charlton were, quite simply, appalling and, when Junior McDougald put Dagenham ahead shortly before half-time, it looked as though they would become the first non-league club to beat a Premiership side in the FA Cup. With four minutes left, and thousands of red-faced Addicks fans scurrying for the exits, a John Salako shot took a wicked deflection past Daggers' keeper Tony Roberts. It was a get-out-of-jail card of massive and undeserved proportions for Jekyll and Hyde Charlton.

MONDAY 7th JANUARY 1946

You get to the FA Cup Final by not losing a game during the earlier rounds, right? Well, wrong actually, as Charlton proved in 1946. For one season the cup was played over two legs between the first round and the quarter-finals. 35,000 saw Charlton beat Fulham 3-1 at The Valley on the 5th of January and, two days later, the sides met again at Craven Cottage. This time Fulham triumphed 2-1, but Charlton still went on to reach Wembley.

SATURDAY 7th JANUARY 1956

Charlton were installed as favourites to win the FA Cup after the club's record victory in the competition, as Burton Albion were beaten 7-0 at The Valley. The performance won praise from Albion's player-coach, ex-Derby County striker Jackie Stamps, who said: "Jimmy Seed's boys have such goal thrust." The game was played in rapidly fading light, and Burton keeper Bill Townsend said wistfully: "I couldn't see the ball until it was flashing past me."

WEDNESDAY 8th JANUARY 1969

A fine season for Charlton included a memorable FA Cup third-round replay victory at Crystal Palace in front of almost 40,000. First, Ray Treacy controlled a Matt Tees header and swivelled before smashing the ball into the net. His second, a minute before half-time, was even better. Graham Moore cleared, Tees helped it on and Treacy hared goalwards before blasting the ball past the advancing John Jackson to make it 2-0.

TUESDAY 9th JANUARY 1979

Boxing in the 1970s was about over-hyped bouts between star names. Ali v Foreman, Ali v Frazier and....Hales v Flanagan. The Charlton 'striking' partners engaged in a stand-up fist fight during a third-round cup tie against Maidstone United. After 86 minutes, the pair traded insults, after which Hales lashed out twice at Flanagan, who responded with a punch of his own. Referee Brian Martin said: "I had to consult a linesman to confirm what I had seen, then had no alternative but to send them both off." The fight made national headlines, and manager Andy Nelson called it "the most serious breach of discipline in the club's history". Hales's contract was immediately terminated.

SATURDAY 10th JANUARY 1998

The highest league crowd at The Valley for nearly 17 years saw Charlton see off one of their main rivals, Middlesbrough, in this promotion-winning year. The home sections were completely sold out and many Charlton fans in the 15,729 crowd had to sit among the Boro fans in the Jimmy Seed Stand. Charlton brushed the Teesiders aside 3-0 and sent out a strong message to their other main rivals – Nottingham Forest, Sunderland and Ipswich Town.

SATURDAY 11th JANUARY 2003

When you play at one of the richest football clubs on the planet you have a right to expect a decent playing surface. But when Charlton ran out at Stamford Bridge before today's Premiership match against Chelsea they were horrified to discover a pitch more akin to Bondai Beach. Chelsea were due to lay a new pitch after the game and had made preparations by covering the surface with tons of sand. Charlton, who lost 4-1, formally requested that the game should be replayed on grass in accordance with Premiership rules. Chelsea were later fined £5,000 for failing to inform Charlton of the state of the pitch beforehand.

SUNDAY 12th JANUARY 1975

Some players are so good that their team is noticeably poorer in their absence. One such player was Richard Rufus, born on this day in 1975. Rufus made his full debut at Roker Park in November 1994. After the game, a Sunderland director told Alan Curbishley: "I've just seen a future England centre-half – that Rufus is one hell of a player." However, despite repeated calls, Rufus never got the cap his superlative performances deserved. His premature retirement through injury robbed Charlton of a great talent.

SATURDAY 13th JANUARY 1923

After Charlton saw off Northampton Town and Darlington in the qualifying rounds of the FA Cup, they landed mighty Manchester City in the first-round proper. City were hot favourites to win but Charlton upset the form books with a 2-1 win thanks to goals from Bert Goodman and Arthur Whalley. Whalley was the undoubted man of the match, with one reporter saying: "He was one of the most virile players on the field. He tackled valiantly and fed his forwards with the nicest precision."

TUESDAY 13th JANUARY 1981

If you fancied doing a spot of DIY back in the 1970s, then you might have popped down to your local FADS store. The Orpington-based firm was one of the largest paint and wallpaper firms in the country and the firm's chief executive, Malcolm Stanley, was a lifelong Charlton fan. When the Addicks were seeking their first ever sponsorship deal, they chose FADS. The deal was launched on this day, and Charlton shirts bearing the FADS logo were worn for the first time against Plymouth Argyle on 31 January.

FRIDAY 14th JANUARY 2011

Chris Powell – one of the most popular players to represent Charlton in recent times – was unveiled as the club's new manager on this day, returning for his fourth spell at the club, officially taking over on the 17th of January. He said: "I want to be part of a brighter future for everyone connected with Charlton." Chairman Michael Slater said: "Chris has natural leadership ability and his passion for the club, together with his football knowledge and ideas for the future, are hugely impressive."

MONDAY 15th JANUARY 1979

Following the astonishing bust-up between Derek Hales and Mike Flanagan, it was almost forgotten that the third-round cup tie against Maidstone United had finished all square. Despite the footballing pugilists having no chance of appearing, there was massive interest in the replay and 10,591 – a record for Maidstone – crammed into the London Road stadium. Goals from David Campbell and Martin Robinson were enough to earn the Addicks a 2-1 victory.

SATURDAY 16th JANUARY 1988

On the day Charlton travelled to Nottingham Forest, a new fanzine was launched. Nothing too exciting about that, except this fanzine had a single, clear agenda – to get Charlton back to The Valley. Called *Voice of The Valley*, it immediately disassociated itself from the club and the official supporters' club and ploughed its own furrow. Spearheaded by politics graduate Rick Everitt and Steve Dixon, it was original, inventive and intelligent and, in conjunction with the *South East London Mercury*, was instrumental in helping the club return to The Valley. It would run for 104 issues across a period of almost 14 years.

FRIDAY 17th JANUARY 1975

The 26,104 attendance for this Friday night derby against Crystal Palace was the highest for a league match at The Valley since the final game of the 1971/72 season against Millwall. A Derek Hales goal after 34 minutes secured the win and moved Charlton into second place in Division Three. Delighted boss Andy Nelson said: "We are halfway there, but I don't want to talk about promotion yet."

SUNDAY 17th JANUARY 1999

With added time looming at The Valley against Newcastle United, Charlton were facing the prospect of creating an unwanted statistic. The previous week's 3-1 defeat at Southampton was their eighth successive league reverse and equalled the worst-ever losing run in the Premiership by any club. In the 90th minute Charlton trailed 2-1 before Martin Pringle squeezed a left foot shot in past Steve Harper to send The Valley into raptures. It was only a draw but the celebrations were long and heartfelt.

SATURDAY 18th JANUARY 1969

A goal described by hard man Dave Mackay as 'a goal in a million' ended Derby County's 13-match unbeaten run. The Rams, managed by Brian Clough, came to The Valley as hot favourites to win promotion to the First Division, but were undone by Ray Treacy's 75th-minute gem. Alan Campbell swept a long pass out to the right from where Bob Curtis crossed first time. It was met by Treacy who volleyed the ball gloriously past Les Green. Five minutes later, Matt Tees headed a second to give Charlton an eye-catching victory in front of 30,115 fans.

SATURDAY 18th JANUARY 1992

Newcastle United again, this time at St James' Park, and an even better comeback with a stunning finale. The struggling Magpies raced out of the blocks and, after just 34 minutes, led 3-0, with victory surely inevitable. But a fine strike from left-back Anthony Barness before half-time gave Charlton a sniff. After the break, the Addicks poured forward. On 73, Colin Walsh made it 3-2 and then, three minutes later, grabbed an equaliser. In the final minute, Alan Pardew scored with a deflected effort to complete Charlton's greatest comeback in an away league match.

SATURDAY 19th JANUARY 1963

This was the winter to end all winters, with only 1947 vying for the harshest of the century. From mid-December until well into March Britain froze and the football calendar was decimated. On the 19th of January, Southampton came to The Valley as clubs desperately tried to stage some games. At half-time, with Charlton leading 1-0 through a Brian Kinsey goal, more snow began to fall and, after 57 minutes, Yorkshire referee Peter Rhodes said: "That's enough lads. I can't see the lines anymore." Just one game would be played in the next six weeks.

SATURDAY 20th JANUARY 2007

Charlton – never the best of travellers – went away-win crazy at the start of the 2005/06 season, winning their first five away games. They then very quickly reverted to type and developed a particularly nasty bout of travel sickness. It took 15 months and 25 matches before they picked up more than a point away from The Valley. Before today's game at Portsmouth, they'd taken just five points from a possible 75 on the road. But a 79th-minute goal from Amdy Faye – his first in English football - secured a 1-0 victory at Fratton Park.

SATURDAY 21st JANUARY 1961

Charlton boss Jimmy Trotter berated stay-away fans after another Valley goal-fest as the Addicks crushed Swansea Town 6-2. A hat-trick from Sam Lawrie, two from Stuart Leary and one from Johnny Summers saw off the Swans. Charlton's previous 12 games had seen 69 goals scored and Trotter said: "We've had 47 goals at The Valley in seven games and yet we still get a 9,000 crowd. What more do the fans want?"

SATURDAY 21st JANUARY 1978

During the mid to late 1970s goals were almost guaranteed at The Valley. Charlton had a reputation for being brilliant going forward but also prone to shipping goals at the back. On the 6th of April 1974, Charlton drew 0-0 at home to Bournemouth, but followed that with almost four years of football in SE7 without a match ending goalless. It wasn't until January 1978, and today's home game against Luton Town, that another goalless draw occurred.

AMDY FAYE SCORES HIS FIRST GOAL IN ENGLISH FOOTBALL AT FRATTON PARK IN JANUARY 2007

THURSDAY 22nd JANUARY 1914

The term 'legend' is applied too easily, but there is no dispute that Charlton goalkeeper Sam Bartram deserves the accolade. Born on this day in Simonside, County Durham, Sam signed for Charlton in September 1934 and went on to make a record 623 league and cup appearances. Between September 1935 and his final match in March 1956, Bartram played in 561 of the possible 578 league matches and all 44 cup ties.

WEDNESDAY 22nd JANUARY 2003

A man-of-the-match performance from Scott Parker inspired Charlton to a 4-2 win over West Ham United at The Valley. Quite simply, Parker was magnificent, scoring two cracking goals and bossing the midfield. A Richard Rufus own goal had put the Hammers ahead after 19 minutes, but a wonderful free kick by Claus Jensen restored parity after 42. Radostin Kishishev completed the scoring to seal Charlton's 200th home win in top-flight football.

SATURDAY 23rd JANUARY 1988

Low attendances were a constant issue during Charlton's awkward tenancy at Selhurst Park, but there was no such concern on this day, when Liverpool were the visitors. The flamboyance of the away side, containing artisans such as John Barnes and Peter Beardsley, had drawn massive crowds wherever they played, and the traffic came to a standstill as 28,095 packed the ground. Charlton were no match for Liverpool who triumphed 2-0, inspired by an exceptional performance from Barnes. The attendance would remain Charlton's highest during their stay at Palace.

SATURDAY 24th JANUARY 1970

A bumper crowd of 30,300 witnessed an FA Cup thriller at The Valley against Queens Park Rangers. Charlton went 2-0 up within 23 minutes thanks to goals from Gordon Riddick and Harry Gregory. Mercurial Rangers striker Rodney Marsh then took the game by the scruff of the neck and scored on 28 and 33 to draw the sides level. A brilliant, pulsating match went Rangers' way with nine minutes left when Frank Clarke scored the winner. But Charlton boss Eddie Firmani said after the game: "The only difference between the two sides was Rodney Marsh." Watching from the sidelines was injured Charlton goalkeeper Charlie Wright, who said: "If the final at Wembley is better than that, I hope I'm there to see it."

SATURDAY 25th JANUARY 1969

If a header from Charlton's lion-hearted striker Matt Tees had not struck a post at Highbury during this fourth-round FA Cup tie then a major shock could have been on the cards. Arsenal's line-up included future double-winners Bob Wilson, Peter Storey, Bob McNab, Frank McLintock, Peter Simpson, John Radford and unused substitute George Armstrong. On 70 minutes, Tees's superb header hit the upright following a cross from Bob Curtis. But minutes later Arsenal winger Jimmy Robertson scored a brilliant goal, adding to Jon Sammels's opener to make the tie safe.

SATURDAY 26th JANUARY 1952

It's not often when a team concedes six that the goalkeeper wins praise but that's what happened after Charlton suffered a pasting in the North East. After a 6-0 defeat at Newcastle United, reporter George Taylor wrote: "It might have been 26 but for Sam Bartram." Another reporter quoted a Newcastle fan who after the game commented dryly: "There's nowt in team bar Sam Bartram!"

TUESDAY 26th JANUARY 1965

Former Charlton striker Jimmy Gauld was jailed for four years and ordered to pay costs of £5,000 for his leading role in the betting and match-fixing scandal which rocked football in the 1960s. At the end of a two-week trial at Nottinghamshire Assizes, the judge, Mr Justice Lawton, told Gauld: "I cannot forget the thousands of ordinary citizens who...paid their shillings to see football played by what they thought were experts. But for their shillings they got not a match, but a dishonest charade." Gauld appeared 49 times for Charlton, scoring 22 goals.

SATURDAY 27th JANUARY 1990

Lennie Lawrence was brutally honest after First Division Charlton were bundled out of the cup by Second Division West Bromwich Albion. Albion won the game with a freak goal by Tony Ford, whose shot deflected in off a huge puddle. Lawrence gave those people who thought Charlton were unlucky short shrift, saying: "We did not go out because we were unlucky, we went out because we couldn't score. Two shots from Colin Walsh hit the post because they weren't directed well enough and he missed a penalty. Any other First Division team would be in the fifth round, but not us."

SATURDAY 27th JANUARY 2001

When Charlton made the short trip across the Thames to Dagenham and Redbridge in the two sides' FA Cup third-round replay, it marked Alan Curbishley's 500th match as manager. Three weeks earlier, The Daggers had been minutes away from becoming the first non-league side to have beaten a Premiership side in the FA Cup. The replay was equally hard-fought and Charlton edged through thanks to a Shaun Newton goal in the first minute of extra time.

WEDNESDAY 28th JANUARY 1959

An incredible 74,482 'watched' a fourth-round FA Cup replay between Everton and Charlton. How many of those actually saw anything is another matter. Liverpool was engulfed in thick fog and one reporter wrote: "This was the night when the Goodison Park floodlights, claimed to be the most powerful in the country, were reduced to the power of candles." It was 1-1 after 90 minutes but the Toffees went into overdrive in extra time and won 4-1, prompting Charlton boss Jimmy Trotter to say: "The players appeared to have difficulty in distinguishing the different-coloured shirts."

SATURDAY 28th JANUARY 1989

In the build-up to today's fourth-round FA Cup tie against GM Vauxhall Conference side Kettering Town, there had been much talk that The Poppies' fans would outnumber Charlton fans inside Selhurst Park. Kettering played marvellously and Charlton were made to battle hard for a slender 2-1 win. It was estimated that 8,000 Kettering fans attended and there was wry laughter when the attendance of 16,001 was announced. Was somebody somewhere determined that the home side's support would not be outnumbered?

SATURDAY 29th JANUARY 1977

Notts County winger Dave Smith was left feeling very silly after giving away an extraordinary penalty at The Valley. As Charlton left-back Phil Warman surged into the area he was brought down by Pedro Richards. Though Salisbury referee Tony Glasson waved play on, Smith clearly thought it was a penalty and proceeded to pick the ball up. This meant he had committed handball in the area and Glasson had no choice but to award a penalty which Bob Curtis promptly converted to earn Charlton a 1-1 draw.

SHAUN NEWTON EDGES CHARLTON THROUGH A TRICKY FA CUP REPLAY AT DAGENHAM & REDBRIDGE IN JANUARY 2001

SATURDAY 29th JANUARY 2000

A brilliant comeback at Highfield Road saw Charlton overcome Premiership side Coventry City in a fifth-round FA Cup thriller. The Addicks were in a superb run of form but two early goals from City's Cedric Roussel looked to have ended their interest in the cup. Charlton, though, had other ideas. Two quick goals from John Robinson and Shaun Newton just before the break levelled the scores. With two minutes left, and a large away contingent roaring them on, Charlton broke swiftly. In a move involving Martin Pringle and Andy Todd, the ball finally found its way to Andy Hunt and he managed to squeeze the ball past City keeper Magnus Hedman to secure an unlikely victory and complete a memorable day for the travelling Addicks.

TUESDAY 30th JANUARY 2001

Claus Jensen joined Charlton in July 2000 and quickly earned a reputation with fans as a highly-skilled box-to-box playmaker. If ever these qualities were encapsulated in one moment it was with a brilliant piece of skill in tonight's Premiership game against Derby County. With the score at one-apiece, Jensen gathered the ball deep in Charlton territory and embarked on a superb 80-yard run taking him the length of the pitch and past several befuddled Derby defenders. The crowd held its breath as the Dane continued and prepared to score what would have been one of the all-time great individual goals. Though Jensen was denied by Mart Poom in the Derby goal, Scott Parker, following up, slotted home the winner.

SATURDAY 31st JANUARY 2004

Charlton boss Alan Curbishley was an angry man after midfield dynamo Scott Parker was finally unveiled as a £10m Chelsea player following a protracted, messy and ultimately acrimonious transfer saga. Curbishley said: "I am not happy at all with the way things have been conducted over the past three weeks by a lot of people, including Scott." But Parker said that, while he loved his time at Charlton, he needed to move on: "It's an opportunity to become a better player," he said. "You weigh up the pluses and minuses and the pluses outweighed the minuses." Parker made just 15 appearances for Chelsea before being transferred to Newcastle United in 2005 and West Ham United in 2007.

CHARLTON ATHLETIC
On This Day

FEBRUARY

SATURDAY 1st FEBRUARY 2003

To paraphrase Oscar Wilde, to concede one own goal is unfortunate but to concede two looks like carelessness. So the antics of Sunderland AFC would have left even the great Irish lyricist lost for words when the Black Cats somehow contrived to concede three own goals in just eight absurd minutes at the Stadium of Light. First, Stephen Wright steered a weak Mark Fish shot into the net. Five minutes later, keeper Thomas Sorensen saved Chris Powell's shot, only for it to rebound off Michael Procter and into the net. Three minutes later, a Jensen corner cannoned in off Procter's back. Charlton won 3-1 and boss Alan Curbishley said: "I have never been involved in a game like that. Truly unbelievable."

TUESDAY 1st FEBRUARY 2011

New Charlton signing Bradley Wright-Phillips scored a fine debut winner but all the talk was about a crazy incident which left visitors Colchester United seething. Steven Gillespie netted for the U's after 63 minutes, but referee Darren Sheldrake disallowed it after ruling him offside despite his assistant keeping his flag down. Crucially, Sheldrake had blown his whistle before the ball entered the net. However, after a brief consultation between the officials, the goal was allowed to stand. Then Sheldrake changed his mind again and disallowed the goal. At this point nobody quite knew what was going on. Replays showed that Sheldrake originally made the right call but made a complete hash of communicating it. Wright-Phillips became the 71st Charlton player to score on his debut with a superb overhead kick with 12 minutes remaining.

SATURDAY 2nd FEBRUARY 1924

The inadequate seating at The Mount – Charlton's new ground in Catford – meant that the club received special permission to play today's second-round cup tie against Wolverhampton Wanderers at The Valley. 20,057 fans witnessed an extraordinary miss by Charlton centre-forward Bob Thomson in the first five minutes of the match. Thomson did well to work his way into the area but, with only Wolves keeper George to beat, he sliced the ball wide. A *Daily Express* reporter wrote: "This was Thomson's only mistake but what a costly one for his side. Such another gilt-edged opportunity did not come his way." The game finished goalless.

SATURDAY 2nd FEBRUARY 1929

Wilson Lennox was a Scottish-born forward who joined Charlton in 1927 and whose finest hour was on this day at St James' Park, Exeter, when he scored all Charlton's goals in a 5-2 victory. At the time it was the club's highest away victory and the first time a Charlton player had scored five times in one match. He remains the only Charlton player to achieve this feat away from home.

FRIDAY 2nd FEBRUARY 1990

Don Welsh, who died on this day in Stevenage, Hertfordshire, will always be remembered as the inspirational Charlton captain who proudly held the FA Cup aloft in April 1947. A wonderfully versatile player who could switch from centre-half to centre-forward to wing-half with ease, Don played 216 times for Charlton, scoring 50 times, and was also skipper during the glory days of the 1930s, when Charlton rose from the Third Division to the First in consecutive seasons.

SUNDAY 3rd FEBRUARY 1974

Now unremarkable, Sunday football was once a controversial experiment brought about by exceptional circumstances. The 1970s energy crisis prompted the FA to ask the Home Office for special permission to stage matches on Sundays when there would be more guaranteed access to power. Attendances were better than expected and, on this day, Charlton entertained Shrewsbury Town with a crowd of 7,880 – more than 2,000 more than the average gate – enjoying a thrilling 3-3 draw as Charlton recovered from 2-0 down. Two Mike Flanagan goals and a Bob Curtis penalty earned a share of the spoils.

TUESDAY 4th FEBRUARY 1890

East Street in Charlton has a special place in the club's history, as it was here that the first meeting was held to form the Addicks. It was also the birthplace, on this day, of a man called Arthur Ernest Ellis who worked at Siemens and helped to dig the bowl that would eventually become The Valley. Finally, East Street was also the location of a 'wet and dry' fishmongers shop owned by Arthur Bryan, who supplied the haddock and chips to players of both teams after Charlton matches. And here lies the secret of Charlton's curious nickname – it is, quite simply, a London linguistic corruption of the word 'haddocks' into 'Addicks'.

TUESDAY 4th FEBRUARY 1986

Skipper Mark Aizlewood was involved in two unusual incidents when Charlton entertained promotion rivals Brighton & Hove Albion at Selhurst Park. One minute before the interval, with The Seagulls leading 1-0, Aizlewood 'scored' with a free kick which hit keeper Perry Digweed before entering the net. However, referee Ray Lewis disallowed the goal, saying it was an indirect free kick. Later on, with the score 2-1 to Brighton, Aizlewood took another free kick which appeared not to cross the line. This time, however, Lewis awarded the goal.

SATURDAY 5th FEBRUARY 1955

South African-born Eddie Firmani is considered by many to be one of the finest players ever to have pulled on Charlton's famous red shirt. On this day, Firmani scored five goals in Charlton's 6-1 win over Aston Villa. In front of 23,988 spectators at The Valley, Firmani was on fire, and already had two goals to his name with four minutes on the clock. When he got his fifth – a penalty after 83 minutes – it was his 20th goal in 13 league matches. It was certainly a memorable weekend for Firmani – the following day his wife, Pat, gave birth to a son called Paul.

SATURDAY 5th FEBRUARY 2000

Striker Andy Hunt plundered a superb hat-trick in a 3-1 win at Stockport County. In the previous league game, Hunt also scored three at Norwich City, making him the first Charlton player to score hat-tricks in successive away league matches. It was also the first time Charlton had ever recorded hat-tricks in successive away matches and, because Hunt had also scored three against Stockport at The Valley in September, he became the first Charlton player to score a hat-trick against the same opposition home and away in the same season.

SATURDAY 6th FEBRUARY 1971

Charlton boss Theo Foley described a serious leg injury to influential Welsh midfielder Graham Moore as "a tragic loss at the worst possible time". Moore broke his right shinbone competing for a ball with Blackburn Rovers' Eamonn Rogers, who would shortly become a Charlton player himself. It would be the last game Moore played for Charlton – a tremendous loss because he was a fine attacking midfielder with an eye for goal.

FRIDAY 6th FEBRUARY 2009

Michael Gliksten died on this day after a long fight against cancer. Gliksten was chairman and owner of the club from 1962 until 1982, when he sold it to Mark Hulyer for a token fee. Crucially, he retained ownership of the ground through his company, Adelong. There is little doubt that this awkward arrangement was at the crux of the disastrous events of the 1980s which saw Charlton leave The Valley. However, Gliksten was by no means the sole villain of the piece, and most Charlton observers believe he was cruelly used and scapegoated by the club's subsequent owners to justify the hugely unpopular move to Crystal Palace.

SATURDAY 7th FEBRUARY 1970

These days a player's skin colour is not even worthy of mention but, in the late 1960s and early 1970s, black players were still uncommon. On this day, Steve Stacey, a Bristol-born defender on loan from Ipswich Town, became the first non-white player to represent Charlton. He marked it with a goal against eventual Second Division title winners Huddersfield Town, who won 2-1 at The Valley.

SATURDAY 7th FEBRUARY 1987

When Charlton first began groundsharing with Crystal Palace in 1985, many Addicks fans got lost as they grappled with the built-up streets of SE25. So it was of some solace to discover that it wasn't just Addicks fans who were bewildered. On this day, the coach carrying the Manchester United team also got lost and only arrived an uncomfortable 25 minutes before kick-off. The game ended goalless, thanks mainly to Bob Bolder saving a 44th-minute Bryan Robson penalty.

TUESDAY 8th FEBRUARY 1994

Charlton stole the sports headlines after a stunning fourth-round FA Cup replay win at high-flying Blackburn Rovers. Following a goalless draw at The Valley, the Addicks travelled to Rovers – whose starting line-up included Alan Shearer, Graeme Le Saux and David Batty – more in hope than expectation. But a 15th-minute strike from Darren Pitcher sent 2,000 travelling Addicks fans into raptures. It was the only goal. Boss Curbishley commented: "This is a great achievement for the club," and then added a classic Curbs caveat: "But I'm not going overboard."

MONDAY 8th FEBRUARY 1999

New signing John Barnes was given a great Valley welcome when he was introduced to the crowd before tonight's Premiership clash with Wimbledon. The 35-year-old former England and Liverpool winger arrived on a free transfer from Newcastle until the end of the season. In front of 20,002 fans and the Sky cameras, Charlton triumphed 2-0 with a goal from Martin Pringle and an own goal by Dean Blackwell. It was a vital three points for the Addicks as they fought to avoid relegation from the Premiership in their first season.

FRIDAY 9th FEBRUARY 1979

The on-pitch skirmish between star strikers Derek Hales and Mike Flanagan during the match against Maidstone United on January 9th was described by manager Andy Nelson at the time as "the most serious breach of discipline in the club's history". Charlton viewed Hales's role more seriously than Flanagan's, terminating his contract but retaining his registration. Hales subsequently appealed against this and, on this day, he was eventually reinstated after both the Professional Footballers' Association and the Football League asked the Charlton board to consider a less draconian punishment. Hales was still fined two weeks' wages.

SATURDAY 10th FEBRUARY 1962

Kenilworth Road was the venue for a superb performance by Charlton, producing their record away victory. The opponents, Luton Town, were managed by ex-Charlton legend Sam Bartram who, after the game, paid a huge compliment to one of his former team-mates: "You can forget Jimmy Greaves and Johnny Haynes. For me, Stuart Leary is the greatest forward in the game. He can dictate the course of the match by slowing it down or speeding it up to suit his team." If Leary was the architect of this superb 6-1 victory, then it was Slough-born striker Dennis Edwards who supplied the killer instinct, scoring in the 32nd, 37th and 60th minutes to notch his third treble in a Charlton shirt.

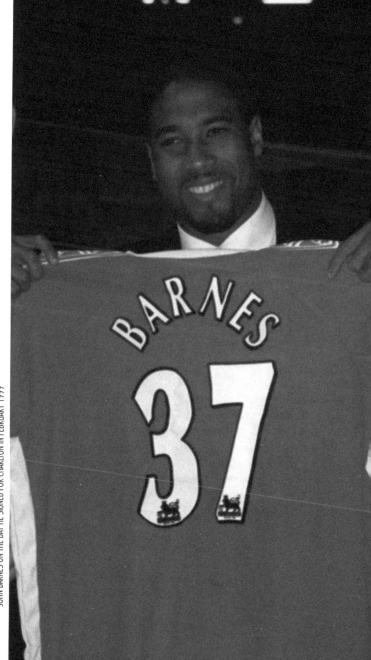

THURSDAY 11th FEBRUARY 1999

Three Malaysian men and a security guard were arrested on suspicion of burglary at The Valley by detectives investigating links in a series of Premiership matches halted by floodlight failures. There were allegations that Far East betting syndicates were behind the problems. The inquiry centred on an alleged plot to tamper with electrical cables at The Valley to blow the floodlights and cause the abandonment of Charlton's forthcoming home match against Liverpool. Despite contingency plans to start the game at 1.30pm, the game went ahead as normal two days later and, thanks to a Keith Jones goal, ended in a 1-0 win for Charlton.

SATURDAY 12th FEBRUARY 1938

In years gone by the FA Cup was always guaranteed to add a few thousand to the gate, but no-one could have predicted the number of fans who would attend the fifth-round tie against Aston Villa on this day at The Valley. An astonishing 75,031 people packed into the ground, including an estimated 10,000 from the Midlands, setting a new record for the ground which stands to this day. Unfortunately, Charlton were below par and the match proved to be a niggly, bad-tempered affair with both sides guilty of strongarm tactics. Villa went ahead following a deft header from Frank Shell on 28 minutes and it wasn't until the 81st that Charlton equalised through George Robinson.

WEDNESDAY 13th FEBRUARY 1946

On their way to the 1946 FA Cup Final, Charlton produced some memorable performances during the one-season experiment where each round consisted of two legs. Brentford were beaten 9-4 on aggregate in round six and Wolverhampton Wanderers were beaten 5-2 at The Valley in round four. But Charlton saved their best performance for the fifth-round second-leg tie played on this day. After drawing 1-1 at Preston North End, they reconvened at a fog-bound Valley and won 6-0, with all the goals being scored in the second half. The star of the show was Chris Duffy, who scored a hat-trick. Afterwards reporters spoke to skipper Don Welsh, who said in his distinctive, slightly shrill, northern accent: "You wouldn't have reckoned we would score six in the second half, would you? We were that much better though."

SATURDAY 14th FEBRUARY 1981

The promotion season of 1980/81 also produced a memorable cup run which finally ended in round five at Ipswich Town who, managed by Bobby Robson, were one of the best sides in the country. Despite losing 2-0, Charlton performed admirably. Manager Mike Bailey said: "This was the toughest draw we could have had but I was delighted we acquitted ourselves so well." Ipswich were being watched by Pierre Garonnaire, the boss of Town's forthcoming Uefa Cup opponents St Etienne, who said: "Charlton were a remarkable side for a Third Division team."

SATURDAY 15th FEBRUARY 1958

Peter Firmani, the younger brother of Charlton hero Eddie, had huge shoes to fill when his sibling departed for Sampdoria. But Peter proved he was a fine player in his own right with a magnificent Valley performance on this day against Middlesbrough. Firmani junior, with just seven league games to his credit, was instrumental in a three-goals-in-five-minutes spell which ripped Boro apart. Charlton led 2-0 at half-time but, inspired by Firmani, went into overdrive in the second half and eventually finished up 6-2 winners, with Johnny Summers bagging a hat-trick.

FRIDAY 16th FEBRUARY 1973

Attendances plummeted after the club's relegation in 1971/72, and the average attendance for the following season was a dismal 5,658. This fixture against Walsall was scheduled to take place on a Friday night to avoid clashing with the forthcoming League Cup Final between Tottenham Hotspur and Norwich City the following day. As it turned out, the final was eventually played on March 3rd, but Charlton stuck to the original schedule to see if fans liked Friday night football. The experiment flopped, with only 5,078 turning up for a disappointing 1-1 draw.

TUESDAY 17th FEBRUARY 1976

At times during the 1975/76 season, Derek Hales was virtually unstoppable, scoring 28 league goals. One of the hirsute goal machine's finest performances came against Fulham at The Valley. 11,551 fans saw Hales score after 32, 46 and 90 minutes to clinch a 3-2 victory. The third was Hales's 50th league and cup goal of his career – 49 of them for Charlton.

SATURDAY 18th FEBRUARY 1967

In the words of Charlton historian Colin Cameron, the home game on this day against Coventry City was the most physical he has ever witnessed. *Daily Express* writer Norman Dixon agreed and wrote of the "bad temper and downright juvenile pettiness"which wrecked the game. Forty-one fouls were committed and Charlton's Billy Bonds and City's Brian Lewis and George Curtis were all booked, the latter for an outrageous barge on Matt Tees which left the Scotsman writhing on the running track. After the game, which City won 2-1, Charlton boss Bob Stokoe described the game as "disgusting" and queried whether Coventry were fed on raw meat. City boss Jimmy Hill described it as "a messy game" and most people agreed that referee Peter Bye had been far too lenient.

SATURDAY 19th FEBRUARY 2000

During February 2000, Charlton were in the middle of the greatest run of form in their history, on a run of 10 consecutive wins. In the sixth round of the FA Cup they faced a tough match at Bolton Wanderers. Thousands of Charlton fans made the trip north and another 5,601 were at The Valley for a live beamback as the Addicks looked to progress to the semi-final for the first time since 1947. Despite an excellent display by Charlton, it wasn't to be. A wonder goal from Wanderers striker Eidur Gudjohnsen and a superb performance from Finnish keeper Jussi Jaaskelainen were enough to give The Trotters victory.

TUESDAY 20th FEBRUARY 1978

Chris Duffy, who died on this day, will always have a special place in the hearts of Charlton fans, as it was his goal which won the FA Cup Final against Burnley in 1947. Duffy always seemed to save his best performances for the cup, netting 15 times in 16 appearances during the great cup runs of 1946 and 1947, including that fine strike against Burnley. A popular anecdote among Charlton fans was that after his extra-time winner, Duffy ran the length of the pitch in celebration. It wasn't quite that far but nevertheless his exuberance – which ended when he leapt into the arms of Jack Shreeve – was unusual for a time when most goals were greeted with a manly handshake and a ruffle of the hair.

TUESDAY 21st FEBRUARY 1950

When 16-year-old friends Eddie Firmani and Stuart Leary stepped off a ship on this day at Southampton, no one could have predicted the lasting influence they would have at Charlton. Jimmy Seed had spotted the pair playing for Cape Town side Clyde FC and decided to bring them to England. It proved a masterstroke as they went on to become two of the finest players to represent Charlton. Leary scored 163 goals in 403 appearances and Firmani 89 in 177 appearances in three separate stints.

SATURDAY 21st FEBRUARY 1976

Goalkeeper Graham Tutt made his Charlton debut in March 1974, aged just 17, and quickly established himself as the team's first choice keeper. But just seven minutes into today's match at Roker Park, Sunderland striker Tom Finney caught Tutt full in the face with his boot. Tutt suffered horrific facial injuries, including a fractured nose, badly damaged cheekbone, double vision and terrible cuts and bruising to his right eye. The photograph of Tutt being stretchered off, right eye a bloody mess, in front of stunned Sunderland fans remains one of the most striking and poignant Charlton images ever. Tutt never played league football again.

SATURDAY 22nd FEBRUARY 1997

A see-saw thriller at The Valley on this day, as ten-man Charlton fought back to draw 4-4 with Norwich City with two goals in the final three minutes. On 28 minutes, Addicks defender Stuart Balmer was ordered off for a professional foul. Norwich pressed home their advantage and, with just six minutes left, led 4-2. But in an extraordinary finale, Jason Lee pulled one back on 87 minutes and, one minute later, Carl Leaburn grabbed an improbable equaliser to send The Valley faithful home highly satisfied.

MONDAY 23rd FEBRUARY 1932

The Gliksten family first became associated with the club on this day. Brothers Albert and Stanley were wealthy timber merchants, and became chairman and deputy chairman at the head of a new four-man board. For the next 50 years the Gliksten family would be inextricably linked with the club before their association ended in bitterness and acrimony and cast a shadow over the disastrous events of the 1980s.

SATURDAY 24th FEBRUARY 1951

There were several brilliant performances by Hans Jeppson during his whirlwind career with Charlton, but none better than his outstanding display on this day against Arsenal. Jeppson scored a superb hat-trick as Charlton swept The Gunners aside 5-2. It was the first time Arsenal had conceded five at home in the league since 1928. After the match, Arsenal manager Tom Whittaker presented Jeppson with the match ball, inscribed with the words: "To Hans, with congratulations on a great game at Highbury – Tom Whittaker."

SATURDAY 24th FEBRUARY 2007

Alan Curbishley's first return to The Valley since leaving Charlton ended in personal disaster and joy for his former club. Charlton quite simply blew Curbishley's West Ham United away, winning 4-0 with a fine display of attacking football. Goals from Darren Ambrose, Darren Bent and two excellent strikes from Jerome Thomas sent The Valley crowd into ecstasy and had the West Ham fans demanding their money back. Charlton boss Alan Pardew said: "I have a genuine love for West Ham and that will never die but we really needed a result for Charlton today."

SATURDAY 25th FEBRUARY 1984

It's easy to be blasé in hindsight, but there was a distinct possibility that today's away match against Swansea City might have been Charlton Athletic's last. Crippled with debts, and facing a winding-up order from the Inland Revenue, there appeared to be no escape. There had been a grim succession of 'last ever' games going back at least six months, though most people were sure the match at Vetch Field, which Swansea City won 1-0, would genuinely be the last.

SATURDAY 26th FEBRUARY 1983

To describe this as a bad day at the office for Charlton would be an understatement of monumental proportions. Today's trip to Burnley resulted in a 7-1 mauling, two dismissals and a bad injury to goalkeeper Nicky Johns. Charlton were already 2-1 down when Derek Hales received his marching orders, and six minutes later he was joined in the bath by Mark Aizlewood for an alleged elbow. Burnley ran riot in the latter stages of the game, scoring five times in the final 13 minutes.

ALAN PARDEW APPLAUDS ALAN CURBISHLEY ON HIS FIRST VISIT BACK TO THE VALLEY AFTER LEAVING THE CLUB, IN FEBRUARY 2007

FRIDAY 27th FEBRUARY 1942

The 1960s was a particularly mediocre decade for Charlton, but one shining light was Mike Bailey, who was born on this day. Bailey turned professional in March 1959 and went on to make 169 appearances for the club, scoring 22 goals. An outstanding half-back, Bailey won two caps as a Charlton player. He was sold to Wolverhampton Wanderers in February 1966, but returned to The Valley as manager in March 1980 and won promotion from the Third Division the following season.

WEDNESDAY 28th FEBRUARY 2001

No Charlton player had represented England since Mike Bailey in 1965 (see above) and there were several cries of 'Chris Who?' when England boss Sven-Goran Eriksson picked Chris Powell for his squad to play in a friendly against Spain at Villa Park. The *Mirror* even ran a picture of Richard Rufus instead of Powell, perhaps demonstrating what an unknown quantity he was. However, Powell acquitted himself excellently, even prompting *Daily Express* writer Shaun Custis to say he was England's best performer, before he was injured, in an impressive 3-0 victory.

SATURDAY 29th FEBRUARY 1936

With the Football League and the promoters of football pools at loggerheads, the League tried to scupper the pools' promoters by keeping fixtures secret until the day before the match. It meant the match programme for Charlton's home game against Swansea City had to be compiled without the editorial team knowing for certain whom the Addicks were facing.

CHARLTON ATHLETIC
On This Day

MARCH

SATURDAY 1st MARCH 1947

Bedridden with pleurisy, Charlton boss Jimmy Seed played a 'lucky tune' on his piano during a sixth-round cup tie against Preston. Seed listened to the match via a telephone commentary. "It nearly killed me," he chuckled afterwards: "My temperature must have rocketed to danger point several times." With Charlton leading 2-1, Seed padded downstairs in his slippers to play the tune. Though he refused to reveal its name, it worked and Charlton were in the last four.

TUESDAY 1st MARCH 2011

Chris Powell made a dream start with four wins in his first four games but then it all went wrong. Defeats against Hartlepool United, Exeter City and Notts County followed before Charlton faced Carlisle United at The Valley. More woe ensued with United leaving SE7 with a 3-1 win.

FRIDAY 2nd MARCH 1984

Described in the High Court as 'hopelessly insolvent', Charlton's likely failure to fulfil tomorrow's away fixture at Blackburn Rovers looked certain to spell the end of the club. On the orders of the Official Receiver, The Valley was locked and it looked likely that Charlton would die. At 5pm came dramatic news that the match had been postponed and the court hearing adjourned until Monday. It was a vital stay of execution.

TUESDAY 3rd MARCH 1970

Boss Eddie Firmani claimed to know what was causing the team's dreadful slump in form after six consecutive defeats, but he was giving nothing away. "The reasons must stay a secret," he said. "If I started talking about it then I think morale would suffer." Whatever the mystery malaise was, it continued tonight with a 2-0 defeat at home to Middlesbrough.

SATURDAY 3rd MARCH 1984

'Charlton Get Last Chance', screamed the *Daily Express*, before saying that yesterday's 11th-hour reprieve came "just as the noose was about to be placed around their necks." The report said a consortium, backed by construction company Sunley, was confident of being allowed to go ahead with a £1.6m scheme to save the club. Consortium solicitor Peter Crystal said: "There are a lot of people doing everything humanly possible to save this club. If it can be done, it will be done."

SUNDAY 4th MARCH 1979

The fall-out from the Derek Hales and Mike Flanagan shenanigans continued and, with speculation about his future rife, the latter vanished. Shortly before this, Tampa Bay Rowdies had put in a bid for Flanagan. It later transpired that Flanagan had taken a break in the Caribbean, furious that Charlton had decided to reinstate Hales. He told reporters: "Charlton have been saying I walked out because the move to Tampa fell through. That is not the case. I left because the club had reinstated Derek Hales. That was the only reason."

MONDAY 5th MARCH 1984

On yet another dramatic day, the Football League was accused of pushing Charlton to the brink of extinction. Consortium member Malcolm Stanley slammed the League for insisting that Charlton repay all their debts before accepting the formation of a new club. "There's not a company in the country who could meet all their creditors' demands in three days," he said. But League Secretary Graham Kelly remained adamant: "Charlton's match on Saturday against Grimsby Town will not be postponed. It will either go ahead with a new company installed or it will not go ahead and there will be no Charlton Athletic in the league."

SATURDAY 6th MARCH 1954

To mark his 500th appearance for Charlton, goalkeeper Sam Bartram was presented with a glorious cake before the league match against Portsmouth. After receiving a silver tea-service from Charlton, Bartram was led to the treatment room by Pompey skipper Jimmy Dickinson where he was confronted with the cake, shaped like a football pitch with 22 small models on top, wearing the red and blue of Charlton and Portsmouth respectively. Sam's day was complete when Charlton won the match 3-1.

SATURDAY 7th MARCH 1992

A superb late goal from on-loan striker John Hendry gave Charlton their first win over Millwall for 13 years. In front of 8,167 fans at Upton Park, Hendry curled a brilliant shot past Lions' keeper Aidan Davison after 84 minutes to send the Addicks fans into raptures. Hendry, who had replaced midfielder Paul Bacon ten minutes earlier, was on loan from Tottenham Hotspur and made six appearances for the Addicks before returning to White Hart Lane.

TUESDAY 7th MARCH 2000

Charlton's 4-2 win at Walsall was their 12th consecutive league win, a club record. Since the Boxing Day win over Crystal Palace at The Valley, Charlton went on to defeat Huddersfield Town, Nottingham Forest, Wolverhampton Wanderers, Crewe Alexandra, Norwich City, Stockport County, Wolves again, Fulham, Sheffield United and Bolton Wanderers before the match at the Bescot Stadium. The win against The Saddlers kept Charlton 12 points ahead of Ipswich Town at the top of the table.

THURSDAY 8th MARCH 1984

Today was one of the most tense, dramatic and extraordinary in the club's history. A desperate race against the clock went to the wire and Charlton were, quite literally, within minutes of folding as a football club. Crippled with debt, the club owed nearly a million pounds and had assets of just £27,900. At the 11th hour High Court Judge Mervyn Davies agreed to accept a package put together by Sunley Holdings, headed up by the late John Fryer with Richard Collins and Michael Norris. Though the club was saved, there was a fatal split between ground ownership and club ownership and it would not be long before the true, terrible implications of this became apparent.

SATURDAY 9th MARCH 1963

A brilliant performance by Charlton keeper Peter Wakeham kept the Addicks in contention until the final whistle against Grimsby Town at Blundell Park. Devon-born Wakeham played a blinder as The Mariners peppered his goal as their centre-forward George McLean gave Charlton centre-half Marvin Hinton a torrid time. Grimsby won the game 2-1, but Charlton's goal was scored by debutant Jim Ryan who became one of 71 players to score on their debut for Charlton.

SATURDAY 9th MARCH 1996

There were 12 arrests and 15 ejections when south London rivals Millwall visited The Valley for a First Division league match. Lee Bowyer opened the scoring for Charlton after just five minutes with a superb, acrobatic finish and Carl Leaburn scored with a fierce header one minute from time to make the game safe. After the game, which was watched by 12,172, manager Alan Curbishley said he hoped to complete the £400,000 signing of striker Chris Malkin, ironically from Millwall.

SATURDAY 10th MARCH 1956

After nearly 22 years' fine service, Sam Bartram played his last match for Charlton on this day. There was a gentlemen's agreement between Bartram and manager Jimmy Seed that he would never be dropped and would finish his career at the top. Charlton won the game against Arsenal 2-0 and, after the match, the crowd poured on to the pitch demanding Bartram's appearance in the directors' box, where he was given a rapturous farewell.

SATURDAY 11th MARCH 2000

All good things must come to an end and Charlton's magnificent, record-breaking 12-match winning run was over when they lost, unexpectedly, to lowly Swindon Town 1-0 at The Valley. Before the game, a bust of Jimmy Seed was unveiled in the club's main reception area in the west stand. On a busy day, Charlton also announced that they would be donating the profit of a matchday raffle to hard-up Swindon so that their youth team could take part in a tournament in Northern Ireland.

SATURDAY 12th MARCH 1994

10,500 Charlton fans travelled north to watch the Addicks meet mighty Manchester United in the club's first FA Cup quarter-final appearance since 1947. With the score at 0-0, the Charlton contingent sensed an upset when giant Danish keeper Peter Schmeichel was sent off for taking out Kim Grant, who was in on goal, in the closing moments of the first half. The euphoric half-time atmosphere among the Addicks fans immediately evaporated when Mark Hughes smashed the ball past John Vaughan a minute after the restart. Despite only having ten men, United then ripped Charlton apart, spearheaded by the brilliant Andrei Kanchelskis, who scored twice. Carl Leaburn notched a late consolation for Charlton.

SATURDAY 13th MARCH 2010

Charlton boss Phil Parkinson warned his players to expect a long, tough week of training after going down 4-0 at promotion rivals and London neighbours Millwall. In what was a massive setback in Charlton's quest to gain automatic promotion from League One at the first attempt, the Addicks were swept aside by The Lions, with striker Steve Morison scoring twice. Parkinson said: "It was our worst performance of the season and no-one is hurting more than I am."

SATURDAY 14th MARCH 1981

It's hard enough going to Sheffield United at the best of times. When you're forced to wear the colours of The Blades' arch-enemies Sheffield Wednesday, you know you're going to have your work cut out. At the last minute, after a match at nearby Rotherham United was called off, the television cameras headed to Bramall Lane. Because Charlton only had shirts bearing the logo of club sponsors FADS – which could not be shown – they had to wear Wednesday colours. Goals from Paul Walsh and Derek Hales were not enough to prevent a 3-2 victory for United.

SATURDAY 15th MARCH 1969

Charlton stayed in the Second Division promotion hunt with a crucial 1-0 win at Norwich City. New signing Ray Crawford escaped the tight marking of City's Ken Mallender to head home a Bob Curtis free kick in the 57th minute. The midfield artistry of the increasingly impressive Alan Campbell and the 'generalship' of Graham Moore were the crucial factors in the win according to reporter Marshall Fallows.

SATURDAY 15th MARCH 1975

Charlton have long enjoyed an excellent reputation for their community involvement and charity work. Back in 1975, centre-forward Arthur Horsfield took an interest in the case of Vincent Watters, a 15-year-old fan who needed a kidney machine. Horsfield coached football at St Austen's School, Charlton, where Vincent was a pupil, and set about trying to raise £2,000 for the machine to be installed at the youngster's Brockley home. Before today's game against Southend United, left-back Mark Penfold made his contribution to the Arthur Horsfield Kidney Machine Fund by seeing how far he could throw a football. Fans were invited to sponsor every yard that Mark could throw.

WEDNESDAY 16th MARCH 2005

A superb fourth-minute goal from Jerome Thomas kept alive Charlton's dream of qualifying for Europe and set up a 2-0 victory over Tottenham Hotspur at The Valley. Thomas arrowed an unstoppable 30-yard howitzer past Spurs keeper Paul Robinson, which was greeted with stunned disbelief before the Charlton fans erupted. Five minutes from time Danny Murphy sealed victory, firing home a free kick from the edge of the box to make it 43 points from 29 games for Charlton.

JEROME THOMAS CELEBRATES A FAMOUS GOAL AT THE VALLEY IN MARCH 2005

SATURDAY 17th MARCH 2001

If Alan Curbishley had told his charges to "keep it tight" in the early stages against Leeds United at The Valley, then his words fell on deaf ears. Aussie striker Mark Viduka took just 11 seconds to breach the Addicks' defence. It was a bad-tempered affair which the feisty Yorkshire side won 2-1. Curbs was not a happy man at the end and told reporters: "There were two bad challenges on Scott Parker and both of them should have resulted in sendings-off." Defending his 'babies', Leeds boss David O'Leary replied: "No one was over-physical."

SUNDAY 18th MARCH 2007

On his full debut for Charlton, Chinese midfielder Zheng Zhi grabbed the headlines – and a bagful of tabloid puns – as he played a starring role to help beat Newcastle United. First Zhi reacted quickly to nod home after a Darren Bent free kick which struck the bar. Then, three minutes from time, Zhi was bundled over in the area and Jerome Thomas converted the penalty. "His technical ability is an asset and now he is finding his feet we are reaping the benefit," said boss Alan Pardew.

SUNDAY 19th MARCH 2000

Despite being a Sunday lunchtime kick-off, a top of the table clash, at Maine Road against promotion rivals Manchester City, attracted 32,139 fans on this day, including around 2,000 from Charlton. Though their 12-match winning run had ended against Swindon Town the week before, Charlton were running away with the First Division. Bermudan striker Shaun Goater gave City the lead on 32 minutes, but 11 minutes later Shaun Newton equalised. The 1-1 draw, on a match shown live on Sky, extended Charlton's lead at the top of the division to 13 points.

SATURDAY 20th MARCH 1982

An excellent run of form came crashing to a halt on an artificial pitch. Before Charlton's visit to QPR, they had taken 24 points from a possible 36 and were unbeaten in 12, but the controversial surface at Loftus Road was their undoing as they lost 4-0. Afterwards, Charlton boss Alan Mullery said: "The goalkeeping was rubbish and the back four terrible," before adding that it was the first poor game Addicks keeper Nicky Johns had had in 20 matches.

TUESDAY 21st MARCH 1989

A splendid performance at eventual league champions Arsenal earned Charlton a thoroughly deserved point. Addicks fans, massed at Highbury's Clock End, saw Paul Mortimer give Charlton the lead after a fine run by Robert Lee. The Gunners hit back through David Rocastle and a classic diving header from Paul Davis. But on 66 minutes, Charlton deservedly equalised when Steve Mackenzie embarked on a mazy 20-yard run before firing a diagonal shot past John Lukic.

SATURDAY 21st MARCH 1998

The third-minute goal scored by Danny Mills during this comfortable 3-0 win at Crewe Alexandra was the fastest goal ever scored by a Charlton player making his debut.

SATURDAY 22nd MARCH 1980

Addicks boss Andy Nelson conceded that relegation was certain after a 4-3 defeat at Oldham: "That's it," he said, "we are going down. Even if we win all our remaining games we still won't stay up."

SATURDAY 23rd MARCH 1946

A brilliant goal from Chris Duffy – his second – sealed a semi-final victory for Charlton against Bolton Wanderers at Villa Park. The Scot had already put Charlton ahead on 35 minutes when he embarked on what one reporter described as "the crookedest 30 yards on record." He skipped around Danny Murphy, beat Lol Hamlett and then bamboozled Harry Hubbick before beating Hamlett for a second time, jumping over a desperate lunge from Jack Threlfall and shooting past Stan Hanson. Boss Jimmy Seed described it as "the greatest goal I have ever seen."

THURSDAY 23rd MARCH 1989

There was euphoria when Charlton chairman Roger Alwen rose at Woolwich Town Hall to announce the news that every Charlton fan had longed for. Six hundred of them packed the main hall with another 200 locked out, and they heard Alwen announce that the club would return to a refurbished Valley in early 1990. He captured the yearning for home felt by many when he said: "I came past The Valley tonight and I found myself staring at it. All those memories! We had to go back, didn't we?"

SUNDAY 24th MARCH 1946

After the semi-final victory over Bolton, many Charlton fans travelling back to London from Birmingham were given a personal pledge by manager Jimmy Seed that they would receive cup final tickets. Seed showed his class by taking all their names and addresses and guaranteeing that any fan who took the trouble to travel to Villa Park would get a ticket. This was also extended to 404 other fans who had travelled to the game in 12 coaches from Charlton.

MONDAY 25th MARCH 1895

The great Jimmy Seed was born on this day in Blackhill, a small mining village near Consett in County Durham. His football career started with Whitburn and, it was while there, he was spotted by Sunderland, joining them in April 1914. Just as he was being tipped for a first-team slot, World War One broke out. Seed was badly gassed while serving on the front line, an injury which scuppered his career at Roker Park. However, in 1920, he joined Spurs and spent seven fine years there before enjoying further success at Sheffield Wednesday. He was manager at Clapton Orient before accepting the Charlton job in 1933.

SATURDAY 26th MARCH 1983

Controversy was never far away where Derek Hales was concerned and, on this day, he incurred the wrath of Great Harwood referee D Richardson at Middlesbrough. Hales was preparing to take a penalty but then, in order to fox Boro keeper Kelham O'Hanlon, checked his run. Referee Richardson decided this constituted 'ungentlemanly conduct' and booked Hales. Carl Harris then took the kick and missed! Boro won 3-0, a result that would have pleased ex-Charlton man, Malcolm Allison, who was celebrating the offer of a new two-year contract at Ayresome Park.

TUESDAY 27th MARCH 1979

A magnificent opening-minute goal by out-of-form Charlton stunned promotion-chasing Crystal Palace in a bruising Valley encounter watched by England boss Ron Greenwood. Charlton – with just one point from their previous six matches – took an early lead after midfielder Gary Churchouse dispossessed Steve Kember and found Lawrie Madden on the wing, whose low cross was netted by Colin Powell. But the Eagles were soon level, courtesy of a Dave Swindlehurst goal after seven minutes.

FRIDAY 28th MARCH 1980

Mike Bailey was unveiled as Charlton's new boss after the axe finally fell on Andy Nelson. Nelson departed with Charlton anchored at the bottom of the table and relegation to the Third Division a certainty. Following talks with chairman Michael Gliksten, Nelson said he had been at the club too long and should have moved on earlier. "At the end I just didn't have the same influence over the players," he said.

SATURDAY 29th MARCH 1947

One of the great Charlton performances of all time happened on this day when an Addicks side stricken by a bout of food poisoning beat Newcastle United 4-0 in an FA Cup semi-final. The poisoning struck the night before the game at Elland Road, with five first-choice players – Sam Bartram, Don Welsh, Bert Johnson, Gordon Hurst and Peter Croker – all suffering and up most of the night. Miraculously, Charlton were inspired and goals from Tommy Dawson, Hurst and Welsh (2) gave them a memorable victory. The following day's *Sunday Pictorial* said: "Use all the superlatives in the book – you still cannot adequately describe Charlton's performance at Leeds yesterday."

SUNDAY 29th MARCH 1987

Forty years since the Wembley triumph of 1947, Charlton returned to the famous old stadium after reaching the final of the somewhat obscure Full Members' Cup. The match against Blackburn Rovers gave the majority of fans a chance to see Charlton at Wembley for the first time. Rovers won 1-0 with a late goal from Colin Hendry, after which Addicks boss Lennie Lawrence said: "Of course I am disappointed but I am not holding my head in my hands, which I will do if we go down."

MONDAY 30th MARCH 1970

Following a disastrous 5-0 home defeat against Leicester City on Easter Saturday – and weeks of speculation about his position – Eddie Firmani was sacked as manager on this day. The final straw for the directors was Firmani's peculiar decision to play right-winger Mike Kenning at left-back against the Foxes. It was a gamble which badly misfired and was one controversial team selection too many for chairman Michael Gliksten, signalling the end of Firmani's long association with the club.

SATURDAY 31st MARCH 2007

The Valley Express service organised a record 81 coaches to see this vital Premiership match against Wigan Athletic. It was decided by a late, controversial penalty which Darren Bent converted to hand Charlton a Premiership lifeline. Despite the vital three points, it was a poor performance by Charlton, who failed to derive inspiration from a warm-up routine by opera singer Martin Toal before kick off. Manager Alan Pardew said afterwards: "The opera singing was probably the best thing we did all day!"

CHARLTON ATHLETIC
On This Day

APRIL

SUNDAY 1st APRIL 2001

A brilliant Goal of the Season strike from on-loan striker Shaun Bartlett put the seal on a comfortable 2-0 victory over Leicester City in front of the Sky cameras. After 81 minutes, Graham Stuart sent a long crossfield ball into Bartlett's path. Letting it drop over his shoulder, he lashed a stunning, angled volley across Leicester keeper Simon Royce into the net. On Sky Sports, co-commentator Andy Gray drooled: "If you're looking for a goal of the season, this is going to take some beating." Bartlett's strike did go on to win the BBC's Goal of the Season competition, the first and only time a Charlton player has won the coveted award.

SUNDAY 2nd APRIL 1989

Little more than a week after the euphoric meeting at Woolwich Town Hall, there was a wonderful event at The Valley which was rich in symbolism. The Valley had become overgrown with weeds and cluttered with the detritus of neglect and, in an inspired move, the directors asked fans to come and help clear the ground. The fans responded with gusto and, on this wet, cloudy morning, worked like Trojans to clear the ground. Some hacked away at weeds on the huge East terrace, others concentrated on the grandstand, ripping out old seats and accumulated debris. A huge bonfire raged in the middle of the famous pitch and, all the time, the club's anthem, The Red, Red Robin, echoed around the ground. In his *History of Charlton Athletic*, author Richard Redden wrote: "It was one of the most emotional moments of our lives. As we smiled at old friends and colleagues, there was a tremendous sense of warmth and good fellowship. Our Valley lived in us."

TUESDAY 2nd APRIL 1991

Exactly two years after the big Valley clean-up, a vital meeting of Greenwich Council's planning committee took place to discuss the return to The Valley. Some 600 fans were at Woolwich Town Hall for the meeting where Charlton's supporters were represented by Rick Everitt, Steve Dixon, Roy King and Richard Hunt. Despite a number of objections from residents, the application for planning permission was approved by 17 to one, causing more joyous celebrations among Charlton supporters. Charlton were, at last, coming home.

SUNDAY 3rd APRIL 1994

LWT screened highlights of the previous day's thrilling game against Southend United, which saw the new 6,000-seater East Stand opened for the first time. Charlton were cruising 3-0 after an hour, but the Shrimpers stormed back and goals from Jonathan Hunt and two from Andy Ansah after 84 and 87 minutes looked like earning them an unlikely point. In a dramatic finale, Charlton's Alan Pardew scored to clinch the points.

SATURDAY 4th APRIL 1981

Charlton boss Mike Bailey was morose after a defeat at The Valley knocked the team off the top of Division Three. 3,000 seats installed in the North Stand were available for the first time, but visitors Huddersfield Town spoiled the occasion with two goals inside three minutes in response to Lawrie Madden's 18th-minute opener. Bailey believed some players were becoming complacent and thought that promotion was in the bag. "The sooner we realise we still have it all to do, the better," he raged.

SATURDAY 5th APRIL 2003

Charlton boss Alan Curbishley said his side were "so bad it was embarrassing" after being trounced 6-1 by Leeds United at The Valley. It was the Addicks' heaviest home league defeat since February 1931 when they were beaten 7-0 by Everton and the highest defeat, either home or away, since losing 7-0 at Brighton & Hove Albion in October 1983. It was also the highest-ever home defeat in the top flight and the highest home or away under Alan Curbishley. A visibly shocked Curbs said afterwards: "The players didn't look like they knew each other from Adam. It was totally unacceptable."

SATURDAY 5th APRIL 2008

Despite losing keeper Nicky Weaver to a third-minute sending-off – the quickest in the club's history – Charlton's ten men earned an improbable victory at Plymouth Argyle to keep their slim play-off hopes alive. Weaver was sent off for handling outside his area, giving a debut opportunity to reserve keeper Rob Elliot. Jermaine Easter gave Argyle the lead after 60 minutes but two mistakes by Pilgrims goalkeeper Luke McCormick handed Charlton three points. Both goals were close range efforts from on-loan striker Leroy Lita.

SATURDAY 6th APRIL 1929

Castleford-born striker Jack Horton only missed nine of Charlton's 252 league matches played between 1926/27 and 1932/33. In the promotion-winning season of 1928/29 he scored 18 goals, including four in a 5-2 win over Fulham at Craven Cottage on this day. A report in Monday's *Daily Express* read: "Charlton gave an excellent account of themselves. They always looked the better team with not a weak spot showing."

FRIDAY 6th APRIL 2007

Charlton battled hard to earn a precious point at Manchester City, lifting them out of the bottom three for the first time since September. More than 2,000 Addicks fans took advantage of subsidised travel to make the journey to Eastlands, and thousands more watched the game live on Sky TV. The draw meant Charlton had won 11 points out of a possible 15 and clawed themselves above Sheffield United by virtue of goals scored.

MONDAY 7th APRIL 1975

The Addicks strengthened their promotion hopes with a hard-earned victory over Tranmere Rovers. With gale-force winds battering Prenton Park, both sides found the going difficult but after 19 minutes Derek Hales scored from close range. It left Charlton in third place, behind Blackburn and Plymouth, with five games to play.

MONDAY 8th APRIL 1991

An important change took place at board level with the recruitment of two new directors who would both play significant roles in securing Charlton's return to The Valley. Martin Simons – a Lloyds underwriter – and Richard Murray, the chairman of television programme and big screen operator AVESCO, joined the board. Both men injected desperately-needed finance into the club's coffers.

SATURDAY 8th APRIL 2000

Fifteen Charlton fans needed hospital treatment after the coaches they were travelling in to Nottingham Forest were involved in a collision. Some 5,200 fans travelled on 78 club-subsidised coaches for a game which could have seen Charlton promoted to the Premiership. The 1-1 draw meant that the champagne stayed on ice but Charlton broke their club-record points totals for 42- and 46- match seasons by winning their 89th point of the season.

FRIDAY 9th APRIL 1976

Goalkeeper Jeff Wood certainly grabbed his chance after a horrific injury to Graham Tutt at Sunderland, breaking a 49-year unbroken Charlton record by finishing on the unbeaten side in his first nine league games. The record was clinched following tonight's 2-1 home win against a West Bromwich Albion side, player-managed by Johnny Giles. The highlight of the evening was a classic goal by Derek Hales, who dummied and sidestepped past three men before unleashing a shot which whistled past Albion keeper John Osborne.

FRIDAY 10th APRIL 1998

The 3-0 win over Reading at The Valley on this day took Charlton's points tally to 78 – the highest since the introduction of three points 17 years earlier. Goals from Clive Mendonca, Paul Mortimer and Mark Bright secured the club's 19th successive home match without defeat, and Mendonca became the first Charlton striker to notch 20 league goals since Mike Flanagan in 1976/77.

TUESDAY 10th APRIL 2001

The 67,505 crowd for tonight's Premiership league match against Manchester United at Old Trafford was the largest to watch a Charlton league match away from home. Nearly 3,500 were also at The Valley watching a live beamback. An audacious chip from Scott Parker almost gave Charlton a shock lead but it bounced back off the bar with Fabien Barthez beaten. An Andy Cole goal was cancelled out when Mark Fish grabbed an equaliser, but United sealed the points when Ole Gunnar Solskjaer came off the bench to grab a winner.

SUNDAY 11th APRIL 1937

After the Italian national side were ordered by Mussolini to pull out of a game against France at the last minute, it was Charlton who came to the rescue and, shortly after beating Huddersfield Town 1-0 at The Valley, they travelled to Paris to take the Italians' place. The following day Charlton played brilliantly and delighted a crowd of 40,000 with a fine display of attacking football which produced a stunning 5-2 win. Two goals each from Don Welsh and George Tadman and one from Harold Hobbis destroyed the French. The party stayed the night in Paris and were back in London at 5pm on Monday.

MONDAY 11th APRIL 1977

During and after Charlton destroyed their team 4-0, Chelsea fans went on the rampage in what remains the worst ever incident of hooliganism at The Valley. After Charlton's third goal, wood was ripped from a stand to start bonfires on the terraces. After the game, bricks and lumps of cement were hurled through the windows of the Valley Social Club, where hundreds of fans sought refuge. A total of 34 windows were smashed. Bar manager Derek Pearson said: "It was very frightening. We were prepared for trouble but nothing like this." Charlton boss Andy Nelson said: "We are dealing with mindless idiots who cannot take a beating." The violence, which was estimated to cost £12,000 in damage, overshadowed a great performance and a brilliant Mike Flanagan hat-trick.

WEDNESDAY 12th APRIL 2006

Almost 6,000 Charlton fans made the long journey to Teesside for a sixth-round FA Cup replay against Steve McClaren's Middlesbrough to see if the Addicks could reach the semi-final for the first time since 1947. The trip was dubbed 'Operation Riverside' and 3,000 tickets were sold on the first day after the club announced they were supplying free coach and train travel. But the Charlton hordes headed back south disconsolate after going down 4-2 in a game shown live on the BBC.

SATURDAY 13th APRIL 1957

Charlton's gallant fight to avoid relegation and preserve their 21-year status in the top flight ended with a 2-1 home defeat to Burnley. Goals from Jimmy McIlroy and Alan Shackleton ensured a win for the Clarets, but not before 20-year-old John Sewell pulled one back for Charlton, confirming manager Jimmy Trotter's belief that the Brockley-born youngster was a fine prospect.

SATURDAY 14th APRIL 1923

'Charlton's Best! Sparkling forwards trounce Newport County' was the *Daily Express* headline about this five-star performance by Charlton in just their second season as a Football League club. Star of the show was Harold 'Dusty' Miller, who scored a superb hat-trick and, according to the report, 'played admirably throughout'. Charlton's forward line showed 'brilliant combination and pace' and the other goals were scored by Alex Steele, Sid Castle and Arthur Whalley.

SATURDAY 15th APRIL 1944

Future US President General Dwight D Eisenhower was the guest of honour as Charlton won the wartime League South Cup Final at Wembley, beating Chelsea in front of 85,000 fans. Chelsea went ahead thanks to a Joe Payne penalty but Charlton struck back before half-time with goals from Charlie Revell (2) and Don Welsh. Many observers attributed Charlton's win to the defensive work of George Smith and Allenby Chilton, guesting from Manchester United, who between them snubbed out Chelsea's highly-rated wingers Charlie Mitten and Llew Ashcroft.

TUESDAY 16th APRIL 1991

A somewhat dull game against Oldham Athletic at Selhurst Park was drifting to a lame 1-1 conclusion when, just minutes from time, Latics boss Joe Royle decided to throw a bucket of water over a photographer. Lensman Paul Clarke filed a complaint after Royle suddenly leapt out of the away dugout and emptied the bucket over his head.

SATURDAY 16th APRIL 2005

If you want to play Charlton, then the 16th of April might be a good day to do it. Since 1923, Charlton have played 19 times on this date and never won. They have drawn on six occasions and, like the outcome of today's home match against Bolton Wanderers, lost 13 times. After the 2-1 reverse against his old club, defender Mark Fish said: "We perform well when we start but then we start conceding goals as we get closer to the run-in."

SATURDAY 17th APRIL 1915

Despite the outbreak of war, season 1914/15 had begun normally for Charlton. But as the conflict intensified, crowds began to dwindle as fans either joined the armed forces or worked long hours in local factories. In March 1915, the club took the decision to close down because of the lack of players and support. The last game was played on this day – a friendly against a Charlton Charity Cup XI which Charlton won 4-1, watched by just 56 people. In his *History of Charlton Athletic*, Richard Redden quoted the 1927/28 handbook which said that 'the majority of boys had left to take part in the Greater Game Overseas'.

TUESDAY 17th APRIL 1990

After four seasons of brave struggle, Charlton finally lost their top-flight status with a 2-1 home defeat against Wimbledon. The Dons were 2-0 up within eight minutes and an Eric Young comedy own goal – he powered a brilliant header past Hans Segers - was the only bright spot for the Charlton fans. Manager Lennie Lawrence said afterwards: "It is a sad day but we have had four years in the First Division, playing on somebody else's ground, in front of Third Division crowds."

SATURDAY 18th APRIL 2009

Charlton skipper Mark Hudson said the players must shoulder their share of the blame as the Addicks slid to their second relegation in three seasons. After squandering a 2-0 lead against Blackpool at The Valley, the side were condemned to the third tier for the first time since 1981. Boss Phil Parkinson, who oversaw just three wins from 17 games, added: "I knew it was going to be an enormous task when I started, but we have fallen short and that's the reality."

SATURDAY 19th APRIL 1969

A successful season for Charlton ended with a whimper and two missed penalties against Preston North End, who left The Valley with a 1-0 win thanks to a Willie Irvine header. Ipswich referee John Osborne awarded Charlton two dubious penalties within four minutes of each other. They were both missed – first by Bob Curtis and then Harry Gregory. After the game, Charlton coach Theo Foley said: "This was one of our bad days. We didn't play much football at all." But 1968/69 was a good season and Charlton finished third in Division Two.

SATURDAY 20th APRIL 1996

"Draw in a minute, we're gonna draw in a minute!" Well, Charlton fans didn't actually sing this particular song but they might have done because this was the season the team couldn't stop drawing. The 0-0 draw at Reading on this day was their 18th of the season, an all-time record for the club. It was a feisty game at Elm Park which saw 19-year-old Lee Bowyer needing a precautionary X-ray after being elbowed by a certain Phil Parkinson. Charlton eventually drew 20 league games during the season.

SATURDAY 21st APRIL 1979

Evergreen Keith Peacock made his final appearance for the club on this day in a goalless draw against West Ham United. The draw left Charlton in the relegation mire but manager Andy Nelson drew some positives from the match: "We've started to battle at last and we got the first clean sheet in memory," he said. Both sides were jeered off at the end of this dull spectacle.

MONDAY 22nd APRIL 1935

Don Welsh and defender Frank Rist were singled out for praise after Charlton beat Aldershot Town 4-0 and guaranteed promotion from the Third Division (South). Welsh, Monty Wilkinson, George Robinson and Harold Hobbis scored the goals to see off The Shots. The report, in the *Daily Express*, said: "Welsh, famous Charlton pivot, turned centre-forward yesterday. A great success, he scored the first goal in a 4-0 rout."

MONDAY 23rd APRIL 1923

With Charlton facing severe money problems, the directors panicked and concluded that, while at The Valley, Charlton could not succeed. On this day, the board met to formally consider a move to Catford, with a view to merging with the amateurs of Catford Southend, foolishly believing that the new location would attract higher attendances.

TUESDAY 23rd APRIL 1974

Ex-Manchester City boss Ron Saunders was an early candidate for the vacant manager's seat at The Valley after chairman Michael Gliksten announced that Theo Foley had been sacked. Foley spent slightly more than four years as Charlton boss, but relegation from Division Two and then two mid-table finishes in the third tier sealed the Irishman's fate, with his final match being a 3-1 home defeat to Watford.

MONDAY 24th APRIL 2000

A 1-1 draw at Blackburn Rovers was enough to clinch Charlton's first championship for 65 years. The league was won largely due to a 12-match winning sequence between December and March, with Charlton limping over the finishing line. With the title guaranteed, there were great celebrations on the Ewood Park pitch. Promotion back to the Premiership had already been guaranteed the previous Saturday.

SATURDAY 25th APRIL 1981

Charlton clinched promotion back to the Second Division at the first attempt with a 2-1 victory over Carlisle United at Brunton Park. The Addicks travelled to Cumbria on the back of an appalling run which had seen them take just one point from a possible 15. But goals from Paul Walsh and Martin Robinson and a consolation from United's Paul Bannon were enough to ensure Charlton joined Rotherham United and Barnsley in the Second Division.

SATURDAY 26th APRIL 1947

This was a glorious day in Charlton's history as the club won the FA Cup for the first and only time, defeating Burnley 1-0 thanks to a Chris Duffy goal six minutes from the end of extra time. The game itself was by no means a classic and Duffy's spectacular winner was a rare moment of quality. After the game, Duffy said: "I just hit the ball as hard as I could and then stood back. I couldn't understand what the goalkeeper was doing for a second. He seemed to go the wrong way and then – whoosh! – it was in the net." After the game, one reporter said manager Jimmy Seed was so happy he could barely speak and just gripped a hand or arm of his players in celebration. Interviewed by British Movietone News on the pitch afterwards, captain Don Welsh laughed nervously after saying: "We're very tired. We've all got cramp. But it's a wonderful feeling. Thanks." Bizarrely, just as it had done 12 months earlier, the ball burst. Charlton joined Tottenham Hotspur and Arsenal as the only three Football League clubs from London to win the trophy.

SATURDAY 26th APRIL 1958

A do-or-die game at The Valley against Blackburn Rovers, watched by 56,435 people, ended in despair for Charlton and triumph for Rovers. Charlton needed just a point to return to the top flight at the first attempt and Rovers needed to win. Though Charlton got the perfect start when Fred Lucas brilliantly headed home after just four minutes, Rovers raced into a 4-1 lead. Charlton hit back through Peter Firmani and a John Hewie penalty but could not find an equaliser. It would prove a watershed for the club, heralding a 28-year exile from the top tier.

SATURDAY 27th APRIL 1946

Manager Jimmy Seed said he was filled with foreboding ahead of Charlton's first FA Cup Final appearance against Derby County because his team were in what he considered the unlucky dressing room. And the great man's concerns were justified when the Rams won 4-1 after extra time. In normal time, Charlton's Bert Turner became the first player to score for both sides in an FA Cup Final. Shortly after his equaliser for Charlton, the ball burst. Extra time belonged to Derby, who scored three times thanks to a brace by Jack Stamps and one from Peter Doherty. In the dressing room after the game, manager Seed overheard one of the team say: "Never mind lads, we'll be back at Wembley next year." Seed picked up on this and said: "That's right boys, and next year we'll go one better and win the cup." Strangely, Charlton's players each received two medals for appearing in the FA Cup Final. With a global shortage of gold, the team received medals made of bronze, although they did receive ones made from gold some time later when the shortage was over.

WEDNESDAY 28th APRIL 2010

Charlton agreed to sell 18-year-old Jonjo Shelvey to Premiership giants Liverpool, who paid an initial £1.7m for the England youth international with further possible payments depending on domestic and international appearances. On the 26th of April 2008, Shelvey became the youngest ever player to represent Charlton, aged just 16 years and 59 days.

SATURDAY 29th APRIL 1972

Charlton were relegated to Division Three for the first time since 1935, their fate sealed after a spineless display at Blackpool. Author Richard Redden says he can still recall the "look of fear and concern in the players' eyes" as they left the coach on arrival at Bloomfield Road. Though Charlton had steered clear of the relegation zone for most of the season, they slumped in form at precisely the wrong time and confidence was in tatters when they arrived at Blackpool. A disastrous 5-0 hammering followed, confirming the relegation. While supporters were crestfallen, chairman Michael Gliksten was surprisingly upbeat and described the Third Division as an "exciting challenge". He added: "There is no point in being despondent or self-pitying. We must face the future with resolution."

TUESDAY 29th APRIL 1975

A glorious night of celebration at an electric Valley saw Charlton clinch promotion back to Division Two. A crowd of 24,659 saw the Addicks beat Preston North End 3-1 to join Blackburn Rovers and Plymouth Argyle in the second tier. Two great goals from Derek Hales and one from Bobby Goldthorpe ensured victory. At the end, thousands of delirious fans spilled on to The Valley pitch and heard manager Andy Nelson quip: "I hope you realise we only lost our last two home games to keep you all interested." Nelson said he also did not regret refusing a bet from Crystal Palace boss Malcolm Allison that the Eagles would finish above Charlton. "I think we have made our point," he added.

SATURDAY 29th APRIL 2006

Charlton fans arriving at the Premiership clash on this day against Blackburn Rovers were stunned to learn that boss Alan Curbishley would be leaving the club. Curbs and chairman Richard Murray had decided to part company after 15 years. After the game, which Rovers won 2-0, Curbishley received a five-minute standing ovation from the fans who had chanted his name throughout. Choking back tears, Curbishley, who steered Charlton from a homeless, near bankrupt club to one pushing for European football, spoke to the fans and said: "Managers usually get booted out of the back door, but I have been clapped out of the front." After the post-match press conference, every journalist present stood up and applauded both Curbishley and Murray as they left – a moving and very unusual event.

SUNDAY 30th APRIL 1933

Stuart Leary can justly lay claim to being the finest player ever to pull on the famous Charlton red shirt. Born on this day, he is described by club historian Colin Cameron as "a footballing genius", scoring 163 goals for the club in 403 matches. Ironically, it was on this day in 1962 that Leary played his final game for the club against Liverpool. In *The Valiant 500*, Cameron introduces Leary thus: "The author can only give a first-hand opinion of the quality of players who have represented Charlton during the post-war years but has no hesitation in naming Stuart Leary as the best he has seen wearing the club's colours."

FRIDAY 30th APRIL 1993

The football world was stunned and deeply saddened to learn of the death of Charlton player Tommy Caton at the age of just 30. Caton arrived at Charlton from Oxford United in November 1988 and, as a teenager, had been considered one of the finest prospects of his generation. He began at Manchester City before making a big-money move to Arsenal in November 1983. His career at Charlton was curtailed by a series of foot operations. His death was deeply felt at Charlton and manager Alan Curbishley said: "None of us can believe it. Although he couldn't play football any more, he was still a naturally fit man."

CHARLTON ATHLETIC
On This Day

MAY

SATURDAY 1st MAY 1937

Two goals from George Robinson were enough to defeat Brentford at The Valley and confirm that Charlton were League Division One runners-up behind Manchester City. It was the climax of an extraordinary rise by the club which had seen them climb from the Third Division, to second place in the First Division, in just two years. Over 26,000 fans saw the victory over Brentford, and the team was chaired off by supporters at the end. It remains Charlton's highest-ever league placing.

SATURDAY 1st MAY 1943

Charlton's first Wembley appearance ended in humiliation after being slaughtered 7-1 by Arsenal in the Wartime League South Cup. Only a penalty from George Green gave the Charlton fans among the 75,000 attendance anything to cheer about.

SATURDAY 2nd MAY 1936

After a 1-1 draw with Port Vale continued Charlton's astonishing rise through the leagues by securing promotion to the First Division, owners Albert and Stanley Gliksten were interviewed in the *Daily Express* and spoke about their £40,000 investment in the club: "We do not grudge one penny of it," said Albert. "We get as much thrill out of watching Charlton as the man who pays his bob. It was not the financial side that interested us – it was the sport of football itself. It is the greatest hobby in the world." Albert also revealed that he should have gone to America on business two weeks earlier but could not bear to go before Charlton had secured promotion.

WEDNESDAY 2nd MAY 1945

Keith Peacock, who was born on this day in Barnehurst, Kent, is one of the most highly-regarded and popular players ever to represent Charlton. This splendid one-club player made 567 appearances for the Addicks and 24 substitute appearances in a career spanning 17 seasons. A wonderfully talented player who scored regularly, he laid on countless goals for the likes of Arthur Horsfield, Derek Hales and Mike Flanagan. After leaving Charlton, he managed both Gillingham and Maidstone United before returning to his beloved Charlton as assistant manager to Alan Curbishley. After a short stint at West Ham United, Keith came back to The Valley again as honorary associate director, and then technical director.

MONDAY 3rd MAY 1937

Charlton's meteoric rise from the Third Division (South) to First Division runners-up in the space of two seasons was the subject of a feature in the *Daily Express*. Reporter Arthur Simmons wrote: "Clubs with money, like Tottenham Hotspur and Everton, disturbed by their results charts, must wonder at the exalted position of Charlton. I may say I, too, cannot imagine how it is done. Charlton have a knack of squeezing the winning goal. And keeping on doing it. Jimmy Seed and his players have their chins in the air. Proud? Of course they are."

SATURDAY 3rd MAY 1986

Remarkably, despite playing home games at Selhurst Park, Charlton managed to win promotion to the First Division. The achievement was sealed at far-away Carlisle where, ironically, promotion had also been clinched five years earlier. Around 2,000 Charlton fans saw the Addicks win 3-2, including an extraordinary own goal by United's Jim Tolmie. After the game, manager Lennie Lawrence and controversial chairman John Fryer were chaired around the ground by delighted fans.

THURSDAY 3rd MAY 1990

In yet another groundbreaking achievement, Charlton became the first football club to form its own political party. The Valley Party had a single aim – to see Charlton return to The Valley. Spearheaded by Rick Everitt, Steve Dixon and Roy King, the party was led by Barry Nugent and benefited from a superb poster campaign masterminded by supporter Richard Hunt. The Valley Party contested 60 out of 62 seats in the Greenwich Council election, gaining a massive 14,838 votes. As an exercise in demonstrating the depth of feeling among Charlton fans, the election was an unmitigated success.

SATURDAY 4th MAY 1929

Charlton manager Alex MacFarlane was so nervous about the promotion-decider at Walsall that he could not watch the match. Instead, after arriving at Fellows Park, he wished his team luck and walked around Walsall for two hours. It was only when the game was over that a Walsall fan told MacFarlane the news he was craving and he rushed back to join his team. Charlton's 2-0 victory was enough to win the Third Division (South) on goal difference and was the first promotion in an eight-year league history.

SATURDAY 4th MAY 1991

Few tears were shed by Addicks fans as the first team played its last 'home' game at Selhurst Park against West Ham United. It was a flat affair on and off the pitch, a tame 1-1 draw involving none of the disorder some had predicted. The Charlton fans in the crowd simply left the ground and did not bother to look back. Five days later, Charlton reserves played Millwall's second string at Selhurst to conclude their spell there. The exile in SE25 was over, but the soap opera that was the return to The Valley had plenty more twists yet.

MONDAY 5th MAY 1980

A dreadful season which began with a 3-0 home defeat to Preston North End, ended equally dismally for already-relegated Charlton with a 'hammering' across the Thames at Upton Park. Despite West Ham preparing to face Arsenal in Saturday's FA Cup Final, Charlton offered no resistance and were 1-0 down after just 17 seconds courtesy of a strike from Geoff Pike. By half-time, Nicky Johns had been beaten four times and a Derek Hales goal after 85 minutes was all Charlton had to show for their efforts. The Addicks finished the season, rock bottom, with a miserable points total of just 22.

SATURDAY 5th MAY 1990

Two days after the triumphant local election performance, an army of Charlton fans – dressed in an assortment of weird and wonderful garb including Batman and Robin outfits, Pink Panther costumes and escaped convicts – travelled to Manchester United for a relegation party. Despite a turgid game which United won 1-0, the day was memorable for the camaraderie and mutual appreciation of the two sets of fans, bonded by their common wish to see United beat Crystal Palace in the forthcoming FA Cup Final.

SATURDAY 6th MAY 1967

Addicks boss Bob Stokoe said he found it "embarrassing" that so many people were congratulating him after Charlton beat Northampton Town 3-0 at The Valley to preserve their Second Division status. "This whole relegation business is dreadful," he added. According to *Daily Express* reporter Alan Smith, Charlton's best players were Les Burns and John Keirs.

MONDAY 7th MAY 2007

Charlton's seven-year stay in the Premiership came to an end with a 2-0 defeat by Tottenham Hotspur at The Valley. After six seasons of quiet, steady progress, it all went horribly wrong for the Addicks following a series of managerial upheavals. Manager Alan Pardew had almost pulled off a great escape but, in this penultimate game, goals from Dimitar Berbatov and Jermain Defoe condemned Charlton to the Championship.

SATURDAY 7th MAY 2011

Charlton fans the world over could simply not wait for season 2010/11 to end. After reaching the play-offs in the previous campaign, a repeat was the very least that was expected. Instead, Charlton finished the season in 13th place – their lowest league finish for 37 years. Following the final game of the season – a 0-0 draw against Hartlepool United at The Valley – boss Chris Powell said: "The season hasn't gone the way we wanted, but it wasn't for the want of trying. Now I've got to get the right players in to play the way I want them to play."

SATURDAY 8th MAY 1999

A seven-goal thriller at Villa Park, won with virtually the last kick of the match, gave the Addicks a late, albeit temporary, relegation reprieve. Danny Mills fired a last-gasp free kick past Michael Oakes to clinch a 4-3 win for Charlton, who had keeper Andy Petterson sent off with ten minutes to go. It meant Charlton's fate would be sealed at the last home game of the season against Sheffield Wednesday. "I think the whole country wants us to stay up," said Alan Curbishley after the game.

SATURDAY 9th MAY 1987

Boss Lennie Lawrence was convinced Charlton would meet Leeds United in the final of the newly-launched play-off system. On a day of high drama, Charlton beat Queens Park Rangers 2-1 at Selhurst Park to finish fourth from bottom of the old First Division and, under the original play-off rules, play the team finishing 6th in the Second Division – Ipswich Town. "If we do meet Leeds in the final, that is really going to be a million pound game," said Lawrence.

SUNDAY 10th MAY 1998

After a bad-tempered play-off semi-final first leg against Ipswich, Town's left-back, Mauricio Taricco, was left with a broken nose. It followed a post-match bust-up with Charlton's on-loan left winger Neil Heaney. While Ipswich boss George Burley initially thought Heaney had launched an unprovoked attack on Taricco CCTV footage later showed Heaney acting in self-defence after Taricco piled into him with flailing fists. The game was decided by a 12th-minute own goal by Jamie Clapham, meaning Charlton continued their astonishing run of clean sheets. "We've still got it all to do," said Alan Curbishley. "The party hasn't started and my players won't be having a drink tonight."

SATURDAY 11th MAY 1985

On a day dominated by a tragic fire at Bradford City's Valley Parade, Charlton went down 5-1 at Maine Road watched by 47,285 fans. A single Robert Lee goal three minutes from time was all that Charlton had got to show for their efforts. The win ensured promotion to the First Division for Manchester City.

SATURDAY 12th MAY 1967

There was outcry from Charlton fans when 20-year-old Woolwich-born defender Billy Bonds was sold to West Ham United for £47,500. Bonds made exactly 100 appearances for the Addicks before Hammers boss Ron Greenwood snaffled him as part of a major rebuilding programme in London E13.

SUNDAY 12th MAY 1996

Charlton made a dream start to their play-off semi-final against local rivals Crystal Palace when Shaun Newton scored after just 55 seconds at The Valley. But the Eagles hit back and goals from Kenny Brown and Carl Veart gave them a 2-1 lead. Three days later, an early goal from Ray Houghton ensured that Palace won 3-1 on aggregate.

TUESDAY 13th MAY 1919

At a meeting held at Troughton Road on this day, Charlton's newly-elected president Sir Ion Hamilton Benn, MP for Greenwich, told the audience that Charlton had been invited to join the Kent League and a new site for a ground had been found at Floyd Road – The Valley.

WEDNESDAY 13th MAY 1998

On a memorable night at a highly-charged Valley, Charlton beat Ipswich Town 1-0 in the second leg of the play-off semi-final to clinch a place at Wembley against Sunderland. On 36 minutes, Shaun Newton skipped past a couple of Town defenders and then let rip with an unstoppable shot from the edge of the box which whistled past Richard Wright. Boss Alan Curbishley said: "This is the culmination of ten years of concerted effort."

THURSDAY 14th MAY 1987

Eleven years earlier, Charlton again faced Ipswich Town in the play-offs first leg, leaving Portman Road satisfied with a 0-0 draw. Boss Lennie Lawrence said: "If we had beaten Ipswich I would be the first one to say we were lucky." Charlton could have stolen an undeserved win had Colin Walsh not had an 11th-minute penalty saved by Paul Cooper.

FRIDAY 14th MAY 2010

A brave header by Deon Burton gave Charlton a lifeline in a play-off first leg against Swindon Town at the County Ground. Burton just beat Town's advancing keeper David Lucas to the ball to grab a vital goal to take back to The Valley. Earlier, Charlie Austin and Danny Ward had given Swindon a 2-0 lead.

SUNDAY 15th MAY 2005

A John Fortune goal eight minutes from time spelt relegation from the Premiership for local rivals Crystal Palace. The Eagles were minutes from safety, having hauled themselves back into a 2-1 lead after Bryan Hughes had given Charlton a 30th-minute lead. Palace thought Fortune should have been sent off for the handball which led to Andy Johnson's 70th-minute penalty. The fact that it was Fortune's bullet header on 82 minutes that sent them down was a bitter pill to swallow.

SUNDAY 16th MAY 1999

Alan Curbishley admitted poor home form cost Charlton their Premiership status after just one season. Having lost 1-0 to Sheffield Wednesday at The Valley to confirm their relegation and ensure Southampton stayed up, he said: "We haven't won our last six home games, while Southampton did enough in theirs to stay up."

WEDNESDAY 17th MAY 1933

When Albert and Stanley Gliksten invited former Tottenham Hotspur and Sheffield Wednesday star Jimmy Seed over to their office in Stratford 'for a chat', they could not have known the marvellous managerial job this north-easterner was going to perform for Charlton. Aside from a couple of years at Clapton Orient, Seed had no management experience but, beginning on this day, he became by far the most successful manager in Charlton's history, presiding over a stunning rise from the Third to the First Division and FA Cup Final success in 1947. He was shabbily sacked in 1956 and died ten years later, but his name lives on in the shape of the 'Jimmy Seed Stand' situated at the southern end of The Valley and a bust in the main reception area.

SUNDAY 17th MAY 1987

Addicks boss Lennie Lawrence saw his play-off premonition become a reality as Charlton beat Ipswich Town 2-1 to set up a showdown with Leeds. In a bruising encounter, two goals from Jim Melrose in the space of 90 seconds set Charlton on their way in front of 11,234 fans at Selhurst Park. An ugly challenge by Town's Tony Humes resulted in Colin Walsh being stretchered off in the 32nd minute.

MONDAY 17th MAY 2010

There was heartache at The Valley as Charlton lost their League One play-off semi-final against Swindon Town on penalties. Trailing 2-1 after the first leg, Charlton played superbly in the opening half and, at the interval, were 2-0 up on the night and 3-2 up on aggregate. When Swindon captain Gordon Greer was dismissed after 67 minutes it looked like Charlton's night, but Danny Ward silenced The Valley with a 74th-minute equaliser to make it 3-3 on aggregate. Swindon then went on to win 5-4 on penalties with a miss by Charlton skipper Nicky Bailey proving crucial.

FRIDAY 18th MAY 1956

Goals from Jimmy Gauld and John 'Buck' Ryan earned Charlton a 2-2 draw against Shamrock Rovers as they opened a tour of Ireland. The game was played at Dalymount Park in Dublin in front of more than 20,000 spectators.

CHARLTON PLAYERS LOOK ON IN DISBELIEF AS THEIR PLAY-OFF DREAM ENDS IN MAY 2010

SATURDAY 18th MAY 1974

The 16-year-old selling badges and beer to rock fans on this day at The Valley could never in his wildest dreams imagine he would return to the ground in a completely different capacity. But Alan Curbishley's older brother, Bill, was manager of The Who, who headlined at a major rock concert at Charlton's ground in front of an estimated 80,000 fans. The event was a great success and Daltrey, Townshend, Entwistle and Moon returned for another gig in 1976.

SATURDAY 19th MAY 1962

At just 23, Michael Gliksten was the youngest ever chairman of a football club, and he was formally appointed on this day, succeeding his father, Stanley, who had died at his home at Farnham Common, Buckinghamshire the previous February.

WEDNESDAY 20th MAY 1998

Charlton goalkeeper Sasa Ilic issued a 'first come first served' invitation to two nations scrapping it out for his services. Ilic's profile soared after keeping an incredible nine clean sheets going into Monday's play-off final showdown against Sunderland. Ilic, the son of Yugoslav parents, was born in Australia and claimed both countries as his homeland.

MONDAY 21st MAY 1906

Frank 'Tiger' Hill, who was born on this day, managed Charlton between November 1961 and August 1965. Though a very astute operator in the transfer market, Hill's legacy will unfortunately be his falling out with – and then selling – the sublime Stuart Leary.

MONDAY 21st MAY 1951

At the end of the 1950/51 season, Charlton embarked on a tour of Turkey. It was not a success – the players found the climate oppressive and the food greasy. But their main problems were on the pitch. Against Besiktas, the home fans objected to what they saw as Charlton's tough tackling and, after Charlton's 2-1 win, angry supporters hurled bricks through the dressing room windows. The second game – also won 2-1 – was played on this day against Galatasaray, and nearly degenerated into a riot. After the referee awarded Charlton a penalty, the crowd went berserk and began throwing stones at the official and the Charlton players.

FRIDAY 22nd MAY 1925

Billy Kiernan, born on this day in Croydon, was playing for a Bank of India team called Lombards FC when he was spotted by Charlton. In the middle of the Second World War, manager Jimmy Seed signed him as an amateur before he enlisted in the Army. But Seed secured Kiernan's services again in 1949 and the 5ft 6in winger went on to play 401 times for Charlton, scoring 93 times. Charlton historian Colin Cameron considers Kiernan as one of the finest wingmen ever to play for the club.

FRIDAY 22nd MAY 1998

Charlton boss Alan Curbishley was in buoyant mood ahead of his side's Bank Holiday Monday play-off final against Sunderland at Wembley. A relaxed Curbs told reporters: "I'm not too scared because this side is already strong enough to give it another go next year. Perhaps we're not little Charlton anymore. The future for Charlton is very healthy. It would be great if we could just finish it off on Monday."

SATURDAY 23rd MAY 1987

A dramatic, late header from Jim Melrose gave Charlton the edge in a taut play off final first leg on this day at Selhurst Park in front of 16,680 fans. Melrose nodded past Leeds keeper Mervyn Day to set up a tasty second leg at Elland Road on the Monday. Melrose later said that he estimated he had clocked up around 50,000 miles during the season travelling to Charlton games from his Manchester home.

FRIDAY 24th MAY 1963

A nail-biting finale to the season saw Charlton avoid relegation from Division Two and condemn their opponents Walsall to the Third Division in the process. Charlton needed to win the game at Fellows Park to be safe, and Walsall needed a point. With injured Saddlers keeper Alan Boswell taken to hospital and Graham Newton hobbling on the wing, Walsall were effectively playing with nine men. Goals from Keith Peacock and Mike Kenning put Charlton two up before Colin Taylor replied for Walsall. Charlton hung on grimly to ensure their survival, leaving manager Frank Hill a very relieved man.

MONDAY 25th MAY 1987

Charlton skipper Peter Shirtliff said the play-offs were more like boxing matches than football matches after Charlton lost 1-0 at Leeds United to set up a do-or-die replay at Birmingham City on Friday. "There is very little enjoyment in these games," he said. "People are crashing into each other because of what's at stake." Brendan Ormsby's 52nd-minute goal was the decider in the Elland Road game, watched by 31,395 fans. Charlton boss Lennie Lawrence said his team would 'give blood' to preserve their top-flight status.

MONDAY 25th MAY 1998

Quite simply, a day no-one associated with Charlton Athletic will ever forget. The Addicks won promotion to the Premiership in dramatic, extraordinary and heart-stopping circumstances. A quite brilliant, topsy-turvy match against Sunderland finished 3-3 after normal time before the Black Cats edged ahead after 99 minutes. Shortly afterwards, Charlton striker – and Sunderland fan – Clive Mendonca completed what must be one of the highest quality hat-tricks ever scored at Wembley to make it 4-4. Each of Mendonca's efforts was a gem and there was even a first senior goal for Richard Rufus in his 165th match. The penalty shoot-out was barely watchable, so gut-wrenchingly nerve-racking was it. Thirteen consecutive penalties were scored before Addicks keeper Sasa Ilic saved Michael Gray's tame effort to secure Charlton's ticket to the promised land. For those Charlton fans present at Wembley in the 77,739 crowd – and those unable to make it – it was an afternoon which proved that, maybe once in a lifetime, dreams really do come true.

TUESDAY 26th MAY 1998

Charlton fans scattered all over the globe woke up with sore heads and huge grins and had to pinch themselves to be sure what they believed happened yesterday, actually did happen. Many national newspapers carried pictures of the winning team on their front pages and a number of reporters said the match was one of the finest ever seen at Wembley. Veteran *Sun* reporter John Sadler said: "If there was ever a better match than this, then I was not there to see it." Meanwhile fans lined the streets of Charlton and Woolwich to welcome the team home on an open top bus. At a civic reception at Woolwich Town Hall, The Freedom of Greenwich was bestowed on the players.

WEDNESDAY 27th MAY 1998

The only sour note on a wonderful week for Charlton was the news that Les Reed was leaving the club to rejoin the FA coaching staff. So, on this day, the club was given permission to speak to Everton's goalkeeping coach Mervyn Day, who was being lined up as a possible assistant to Alan Curbishley as the club prepared for life in the Premier League.

THURSDAY 28th MAY 1998

Sasa Ilic was rewarded with a new four-year contract for his end of season heroics and dramatic Wembley penalty save. It meant Ilic's wages had more than quadrupled since he broke into the first team in February. Ilic said: "I still have to pinch myself. It is a dream come true."

FRIDAY 29th MAY 1987

A dramatic match took place this evening in which, in the first year of the play-offs, Charlton held on to their First Division status in extraordinary circumstances. The Addicks and Leeds United could not be separated over the first two legs and headed to neutral St Andrew's, home of Birmingham City, for the sudden death decider. Amid a hostile atmosphere in which Charlton fans were outnumbered by almost eight to one, the game was 0-0 after 90 minutes. A superb extra-time free kick by Leeds' John Sheridan looked to have settled matters but what followed next was, for Charlton at least, quite simply Roy of the Rovers stuff. With just seven minutes of extra time left, skipper Peter Shirtliff side-footed past Mervyn Day. Then, four minutes later, Shirtliff did it again, heading home a brilliantly-worked training ground routine to send the travelling fans into heaven and preserve Charlton's top-flight status.

SUNDAY 29th MAY 1994

Highly-rated Charlton left-back Scott Minto said he was privileged to be wanted by two major clubs but plumped for Chelsea because he felt he had a better chance of first-team football at Stamford Bridge. The 22-year-old Minto pledged his future to Glenn Hoddle's side, fearing he would end up in the reserves at Arsenal. Minto, who made his Charlton debut against Sunderland at Selhurst Park in the barely-remembered Simod Cup, became the 500th player to represent Charlton at first-team level.

MONDAY 30th MAY 1921

Less than a year after becoming a professional club, Charlton were elected to the Football League on this day, which was being expanded to four divisions. They were aided by an impressive speech by director Edwin Radford, who told a meeting held in the Connaught Rooms in Holborn that Charlton should be admitted to the league because they were the rightful successors to Arsenal and had strong financial backing from a number of other directors. Along with the Welsh club, Aberdare Athletic, Charlton were elected by a comfortable margin.

TUESDAY 30th MAY 2006

Following Alan Curbishley's resignation in April, Charlton announced a new coaching set-up. It consisted of former Crystal Palace manager Iain Dowie as head coach, Les Reed as assistant head coach and Mark Robson as development coach. But there was controversy at the press conference announcing the new set-up when Palace chairman Simon Jordan issued Dowie with a writ pertaining to the reasons Dowie had given him about leaving Selhurst Park.

THURSDAY 31st MAY 1928

Derek Ufton, born on this day in Crayford, was a multi-talented sportsman and one-club man who made 277 appearances for Charlton and kept wicket for Kent. Ufton made his debut against Liverpool in November 1949 and was a mainstay of the side throughout the 1950s. Ufton would undoubtedly have made many more appearances and earned more than his single international cap if a series of injuries had not blighted his career. Ufton's problem was shoulder dislocations – an injury which occurred on no fewer than 20 times during his career.

CHARLTON ATHLETIC
On This Day

JUNE

TUESDAY 1st JUNE 1982

On the eve of an announcement about new ownership, Alan Mullery quit as Charlton boss saying he could not see the club ever reaching the First Division. Mullery said: "There's just not the money for me to spend here at Charlton and I'm ambitious for success."

WEDNESDAY 1st JUNE 2005

Darren Bent, a £2.5m capture from Ipswich Town who signed for Charlton on this day, said the club's ambition had attracted him. "As soon as I met Alan Curbishley and Richard Murray, I had no doubt this was the club I wanted to join," he said. "I am convinced Charlton can go from strength to strength."

SATURDAY 2nd JUNE 1962

Johnny Summers, who died on this day from cancer aged just 34, was a true great. Loved by fans for his powerful running, his Charlton scoring record of 104 goals in just 182 games speaks for itself. He will always be associated with his amazing performance against Huddersfield when he scored five times as 10-man Charlton stormed back from 5-1 down to win 7-6.

WEDNESDAY 2nd JUNE 1982

The Gliksten family's 50-year ownership of the club ended on this day after chairman Mike Gliksten was bought out by a previously unheard of Wilmington businessman called Mark Hulyer, who became chairman of a much-changed board of directors.

THURSDAY 3rd JUNE 2004

The news many Addicks fans feared was confirmed on this day when Richard Rufus announced he was retiring through injury. Rufus, 29, said: "It is going to take me a long time to come to terms with the fact that I will not play for Charlton again." Alan Curbishley described Rufus as "a model professional who will be sorely missed."

MONDAY 4th JUNE 1928

Alex 'Sandy' MacFarlane became Charlton's manager in May 1925 until January 1928 when he left to take over as manager at Dundee. Five months later, on this day, he unexpectedly returned to Charlton and enjoyed quick success, winning promotion to Division Two in the 1928/29 season.

TUESDAY 5th JUNE 1990

The success of The Valley Party in the local elections gave fresh impetus to the move back home and, on this day, Charlton directors Roger Alwen and Mike Norris met Greenwich Council. "We're all talking and it's all positive," said Alwen afterwards.

SATURDAY 6th JUNE 2009

Charlton chief executive Steve Waggott said relegation to League One had prompted a root and branch appraisal of Charlton's structure to come to grips with a £16m budget deficit. "We have had to look at all strands of the business and it is ongoing," he said.

FRIDAY 7th JUNE 1946

An incredible game took place against AIK Stockholm during a pre-season tour of Sweden. Hat-tricks from Don Welsh and Bill Robinson and a goal from Chris Duffy put Charlton 7-1 up. Charlton then completely took their eye of the ball and allowed AIK to storm back. The Swedes scored six times in the last 25 minutes to gain a highly unlikely draw.

MONDAY 8th JUNE 1981

Bert Turner, who died on this day, was one of the stalwarts of the Charlton side which rose through the divisions in the 1930s. If it wasn't for the war, the Welshman would surely have made more than his 196 appearances for the club. He was part of the 1946 side which lost to Derby County at Wembley and put his name in the record books by becoming the first player to score for both sides in an FA Cup Final.

FRIDAY 9th JUNE 1905

Just north of the Woolwich Road, close to the banks of the River Thames, used to lie a small neighbourhood which included East Street, West Street and Hardens Manorway. As was their wont, football-mad teenage lads from these streets used to enjoy regular kickabouts. Such was their enthusiasm for the game that they decided to form a proper team to play friendly matches against other sides. And so, at a meeting held in East Street on a warm summer's evening on this day, the football club, which was named Charlton Athletic, was born.

THURSDAY 9th JUNE 2005

One hundred years since that humble beginning, Charlton Athletic celebrated its centenary. The club marked this historic occasion by unveiling a magnificent, imposing bronze statue of record-appearance maker and Charlton legend Sam Bartram outside the main west stand reception at The Valley. A special home shirt was also launched and the Charlton Athletic Centenary Awards saw supporters of all ages elect winners in ten different categories including cult hero (Derek Hales), greatest match (1998 play-off final) and a Lifetime Achievement Award (Keith Peacock). A gala ceremony was held where recipients were presented with 'Sammys' – miniature versions of the Bartram statue – to mark their achievements.

FRIDAY 10th JUNE 2005

Charlton chief executive Peter Varney said he believed plans to boost The Valley's capacity to 31,000 were an 'absolute priority' for the club to continue their progress. Varney maintained expansion off the pitch would help propel the club to its next level. "It has now gone beyond just being happy to be in the Premiership. We need to start competing," he said.

MONDAY 11th JUNE 1962

The *Daily Express* reported that Stanley Gliksten's widow, Eileen, had not decided whether to challenge his will in which he left her nothing and his secretary, Miss Susan Barry, £30,000. Mrs Gliksten told a reporter: "I will see both of my sons to ask their advice. It did not come as a great shock to be left out of my husband's will." Her 69-year-old husband, who failed in a divorce petition in 1942 and died in February, left £1,217,549, but duty reduced that by £949,597. His sons, 23-year-old Charlton chairman Michael and director David, received an equal share of what remained after the provision of a family annuity and other minor bequests.

THURSDAY 11th JUNE 2009

Charlton chairman Richard Murray said he was extremely encouraged by season ticket sales despite the Addicks' relegation to the third tier. More than 8,000 fans had bought tickets, prompting Murray to say: "The show of support from the fans is very pleasing and extremely encouraging."

TUESDAY 12th JUNE 1990

There was general dismay when fans' favourite John Humphrey was sold to Crystal Palace for £450,000, which included some money Charlton owed to Palace for maintenance at Selhurst Park. 'Johnny H', as he was known, was Player of the Year in 1988, 1989 and 1990 and was a fine, attacking full-back who was unlucky not to gain full England honours.

FRIDAY 13th JUNE 2003

Alan Curbishley began talks with Ipswich Town midfielder Matt Holland after his proposed move to Portsmouth collapsed. Holland had looked set to move to Fratton Park but the move faltered over personal terms, allowing Curbishley to swoop and eventually clinch Holland's signature.

FRIDAY 14th JUNE 1946

As Charlton frittered away a 3-0 lead at Malmo in a tour match, they began muttering some under-the-breath remarks about the Swedish referee and his poor decisions, assuming he would not understand. Though Charlton won 4-3 thanks to a late Chris Duffy goal, after the match they were embarrassed to discover that the official spoke perfect English and had understood every word they said. He later became a good friend to Charlton because, as the Chief Customs Officer for Malmo, he used his authority to 'not see' the many sought-after goods, which were officially subject to export duty, the party took back to England with them.

THURSDAY 15th JUNE 1995

Charlton split the longest-serving joint managers in football on this day when Steve Gritt was sacked and Alan Curbishley put in sole charge. New plc chairman Richard Murray wanted clearer accountability in the management position and decided Curbs was the best man to take the club forward. Curbishley was quick to praise the role played by Gritt and the professional and generous way he reacted to the decision.

WEDNESDAY 16th JUNE 1954

An unhappy tour of South America ended on this day when Charlton became the first English club to play in Ecuador when they played, and beat, Barcelona Sporting Club at Guayaquil. The tour had been a disaster plagued by broken promises, poor organisation by their hosts, inadequate accommodation and violence on the pitch.

MONDAY 17th JUNE 1907

Charlton Athletic FC were presented with their first ever trophy. After winning the third division of the newly-formed Lewisham League – remaining unbeaten in the process – they received their trophy at the New Cross Hall in Lewisham.

THURSDAY 17th JUNE 1937

In 1937 there was no doubting who Charlton's chief was – that would be a certain Jimmy Seed. But on this day it took on a literal meaning. During Charlton's North American tour, Seed was made a Sioux chieftain by Indians at a reserve in Saskatoon. Chief Little Crow gave Seed the name 'Tapa-Ho-Ksina' which, appropriately enough, meant 'football king'. Jimmy returned the compliment by presenting Little Crow with a football formerly used by Tottenham Hotspur.

THURSDAY 18th JUNE 1987

John Fryer had been suffering from ill health for some time and finally stepped down as Charlton chairman to be replaced by Richard Collins. Fryer became joint president with his business partner, Malcolm Sunley.

SATURDAY 19th JUNE 1937

Charlton's North American tour was a huge success in terms of sportsmanship and goodwill. Unbeaten Charlton won 12 of their 13 games, scoring 72 goals and conceding just 9. On this day, they beat Canadian side Winnipeg 9-1, with Don Welsh bagging four of the goals.

THURSDAY 20th JUNE 2002

Charlton announced a new four-year sponsorship deal worth up to £4.3m with retailer all:sports. It included having the company's name on all team kit as well as sponsorship of The Valley.

WEDNESDAY 21st JUNE 1944

John Dunn, who was born on this day in Barking, was signed by Theo Foley in July 1971 as a replacement for the popular and larger-than-life goalkeeper Charlie Wright, who had gone to Bolton. Dunn was Charlton's first-choice keeper between 1971 and 1974, making 118 appearances. He was Charlton's Player of the Year in 1974 but then lost his place to the emerging Graham Tutt.

MONDAY 22nd JUNE 1998

As Charlton prepared for life in the Premiership, Alan Curbishley signed a player who would come to symbolise everything that is good about the club. Chris Powell cost a club record £825,000 from Derby County but repaid that fee several times over, not just with outstanding performances on the pitch but with his all-round character, professionalism and fair-mindedness. Universally liked, Powell would of course eventually return to the club as manager – to wild acclaim – in January 2011.

TUESDAY 23rd JUNE 1998

West Bromwich Albion striker Andy Hunt became the second major signing to be announced in 24 hours and the first to join the Addicks under the Bosman ruling, meaning no transfer fee was payable.

WEDNESDAY 24th JUNE 1987

Steve Mackenzie's wonder goal for Manchester City in the 1981 FA Cup Final replay has always been overshadowed by Ricky Villa's sublime individual winner. Many Charlton fans, though, were mindful of Mackenzie's goal when he signed from West Bromwich Albion on this day for £200,000. After a slow start at Charlton, Mackenzie grew in stature and became an important member of Lennie Lawrence's squad.

THURSDAY 25th JUNE 1998

Charlton smashed their record transfer fee for the second time in four days, forking out £1,045,000 for 33-year-old Barnsley midfielder Neil Redfearn. Redfearn scored 14 goals for the Tykes in season 1997/98.

SUNDAY 26th JUNE 1892

Dick Upex, who was born on this day, earned himself a permanent place in the Charlton record books by scoring the club's first ever hat-trick in an FA Cup match. In September 1920, while Charlton were still a Southern League club, Upex scored three at The Valley against Catford Southend in front of 3,000 fans in the FA Cup preliminary round.

SUNDAY 27th JUNE 1937

Charlton's successful tour of North America continued with a 4-0 victory over a USA Selected XI at the Polo Grounds, New York. Charlton's goals were scored by Don Welsh (2), George Tadman and Les Boulter.

MONDAY 28th JUNE 1982

Charlton manager Ken Craggs was in bullish mood after landing the signatures of Leeds United winger Carl Harris and Aston Villa midfielder Terry Bullivant, both for £100,000. Craggs, who also persuaded Paul Elliott and Dave Mehmet to sign new contracts, said: "We are going all-out to win promotion next season and I think this proves to our supporters that we mean business."

FRIDAY 29th JUNE 2007

After weeks of wrangling, Charlton reluctantly sold Darren Bent to Spurs for a club record £16.5m. Charlton stood firm while a number of other clubs expressed interest, but finally it was only Spurs who were willing to pay the value that Charlton had set. Bent scored 37 goals in 79 appearances for the Addicks.

SATURDAY 30th JUNE 1906

Ralph Allen, who was born on this day in Newburn-on-Tyne, still holds the record for the most number of league goals scored in a season for Charlton. Allen scored 32 goals in just 28 league appearances when Charlton won promotion from Division Three (South) in 1934/35.

CHARLTON ATHLETIC
On This Day

JULY

FRIDAY 1st JULY 1977

When 19-year-old Steve Gritt arrived from AFC Bournemouth, few could have predicted what lay ahead. 'Gritty' became a crowd favourite, making more than 400 appearances for the club. He was admired for his 100 per cent commitment to the cause and his willingness to play in whatever position was asked of him, including goalkeeper. A fine servant of Charlton, fans even created an affectionate song about him which essentially said that, even though 'Gritty' lacked something in the tonsorial department, the fans still loved him. In 1991, he became joint manager with Alan Curbishley.

WEDNESDAY 2nd JULY 1952

Peter Hunt, who was born on this day in Mile End, was a battling midfielder who endured a difficult start at Charlton but eventually won the fans over and became a firm favourite. An integral part of the promotion-winning team of 1974/75, Hunt made 161 appearances for Charlton, scoring eight times, including an opening-minute stunner against Manchester United at Old Trafford in a League Cup tie in October 1974.

THURSDAY 2nd JULY 1998

Inspirational captain Mark Kinsella signed a new five-year contract, keeping him at the club until 2003. The Irishman was Charlton's 1998 Player of the Year and captained the team which won promotion to the Premiership. Signed from Colchester United for just £150,000 in September 1996, he immediately settled into the side and was a much-admired, goalscoring midfielder. Kinsella, a product of the Dublin-based Home Farm FC, played 48 times for the Republic of Ireland, scoring three times. After leaving Charlton he played for Aston Villa, West Bromwich Albion and Walsall. In 2006 he was appointed development coach at Charlton and worked his way up to first-team coach but, along with Phil Parkinson, was sacked in January 2011.

TUESDAY 3rd JULY 2007

Fans' favourite Chris Powell returned to the club for a third stint as player-coach. Powell first left Charlton in 2004 for West Ham United before returning in the summer of 2005. A year later, Powell signed a one-year contract with Watford before returning to The Valley.

WEDNESDAY 4th JULY 2001

Charlton broke their club record when they clinched the signing of Jason Euell from Wimbledon for £4.75m. Alan Curbishley had been chasing the 24-year-old for 18 months. Euell said: "I have come here to make myself a better player and hopefully get on to the international stage."

FRIDAY 5th JULY 1996

Highly-rated 19-year-old Lee Bowyer became the most expensive teenager in British history when he was sold to Leeds United for almost £3m. The attacking midfielder from Canning Town was Charlton's top scorer in season 1995/96.

TUESDAY 6th JULY 2004

After Richard Rufus, defender Gary Rowett became the second Charlton player to retire through injury in little over a month. Rowett, 30, made only 13 appearances for Charlton following his £2.7m move from Leicester in 2002. Boss Alan Curbishley said: "I'm gutted. Gary had enormous ability."

FRIDAY 7th JULY 1972

Following Charlton's relegation to Division Three, it was inevitable that some of their best players would attract interest from other clubs and, on this day, popular central defender Paul Went signed for Fulham for £80,000. The East London-born defender made 178 appearances for Charlton, scoring 16 goals. He was Player of the Year for 1971.

SATURDAY 8th JULY 2000

The championship-winning medals presented to the Charlton team following the Ipswich Town game on April 29th had, in fact, been replicas. The squad finally received the genuine articles tonight at a special dinner held at the Royal Lancaster Hotel, in central London.

SUNDAY 9th JULY 1978

Mike Flanagan's spell with the New England Tea Men in Boston, United States, eventually had hugely controversial repercussions culminating in that 'raving bonkers' style brawl at The Valley with a certain Mr Hales. But 'Flan' also enjoyed considerable success in the States and, on this day, he bagged all five for the Tea Men in a 5-2 walloping of California Surf, taking his season's total to an impressive 27.

WEDNESDAY 10th JULY 1991

Charlton fans were flabbergasted to hear that popular manager Lennie Lawrence had left to join Middlesbrough. Lawrence had become synonymous with Charlton's trials and tribulations during his nine-year tenure and the press dubbed him 'Houdini' for managing to keep Charlton in the top flight during the wilderness years at Selhurst Park.

TUESDAY 11th JULY 2006

New signing Jimmy Floyd Hasselbaink said he was not going to The Valley simply for a final pay-day. "I feel like a 19-year-old in the body of a 34-year-old," he added. "Like a boy with a big piece of candy." Manager Iain Dowie, who completed the free signing from Middlesbrough, said: "He brings lots to the team. Jimmy has a talisman effect."

SATURDAY 12th JULY 2003

Everybody connected with Charlton was saddened to hear the news that Jane Murray, the wife of chairman Richard Murray, had died. Mrs Murray suffered anaphylactic shock after being stung by a wasp in September 2000. She spent three years in a coma before her death.

MONDAY 13th JULY 1936

Proven goalscorer Ray Crawford, born on this day, arrived at Charlton in March 1969 but soon fell out with the club after refusing to attend a special training session at Bisham Abbey and was subsequently dismissed. He only made 22 appearances for the Addicks but scored seven goals, including a classic overhead kick at The Den in August 1969.

TUESDAY 14th JULY 1998

Former England defender Gary Stevens was appointed Charlton's Under-21 coach. Stevens, 36, would be part of the club's new Youth Academy structure under director Mick Browne and have special responsibility for the Charlton reserve side.

SATURDAY 15th JULY 1899

More's the pity that you don't get names like Seth Plum anymore. Yet Seth, born on this day, has a permanent place in Charlton's record books as the club's first player to win a full England cap, which he gained against France in Paris on May 10 1923.

JIMMY FLOYD HASSELBAINK IS INTRODUCED TO THE MEDIA IN JULY 2006

SATURDAY 16th JULY 1966

As England prepared to go World Cup mad, Jimmy Seed died in Farnborough Hospital, aged 71. Following his disgraceful sacking by Charlton in 1956, the man who spearheaded the club's fairytale rise to the top echelons of the game worked for Bristol City and then Millwall until the time of his death.

FRIDAY 17th JULY 1981

Sam Bartram, a true Charlton legend, died on this day on his way to his Harpenden, Hertfordshire home. He was 67. As well as his remarkable Charlton career, Bartram was also manager of York City and Luton Town and worked as a reporter for the *Sunday People* for 18 years.

MONDAY 18th JULY 1955

After a day of secret transfer talk, Charlton's brilliant South African-born striker, Eddie Firmani, signed for Sampdoria. Following what one paper described as 'high pressure Italian persuasion' Firmani agreed a deal which saw his wages rocket from £15 a week to £150 a week. The Genoan club paid £35,000 for Firmani's services – a record fee for a Football League player – as well as a £5,000 signing-on fee, plus a car and flat.

WEDNESDAY 19th JULY 2006

Charlton striker Darren Bent had already proved he was lethal in the penalty box, but on this day he showed he was also pretty lethal in the kitchen! While chopping bread and onions to make a sandwich, he sliced his finger open, leading to fears that he could be out for up to six weeks: "I couldn't tell you what type of sandwich it was. I didn't get to try it," a shocked Bent said later.

TUESDAY 20th JULY 1982

Charlton succumbed to the inevitable and sold hot property Paul Walsh to newly-promoted Luton Town. Walsh, 19, left as part of a £400,000 exchange deal which saw Steve White join Charlton. Hatters' boss David Pleat said: "If Paul can keep his feet on the ground, he can go all the way." "If I'm going to make it to the very top then I need to be playing in the First Division," added Walsh.

FRIDAY 21st JULY 2000

Charlton smashed their transfer record after completing the signing of attacking midfielder Claus Jensen for £4m from Bolton Wanderers. The 23-year-old Dane was also wanted by Ipswich Town, but said: "Charlton impressed me, from the board to the manager and the fans and the ground."

SUNDAY 22nd JULY 1962

No history of Charlton would be complete without making reference to Colin Walsh, who was born on this day. 'Walshie', a £125,000 capture from Nottingham Forest in September 1986 was, of course, the scorer of THAT goal. It was his sweetly-struck left-footed shot after seven minutes which won the game against Portsmouth, crowning a perfect day for Charlton – the day they returned to The Valley.

MONDAY 23rd JULY 1973

When manager Theo Foley completed a loan deal which brought Derek Hales from Luton Town to Charlton, no one could have predicted the impact he would make. Hales was feisty, rough at the edges and bristling with competitive energy. But most of all he was a superb, predatory striker. From the word go, Hales started scoring and, on October 22nd, Foley paid out just £4,000 to make the move permanent. In terms of getting a bargain it takes some beating.

WEDNESDAY 24th JULY 1991

In a surprise move, Charlton named player-coaches Alan Curbishley and Steve Gritt as their new management duo in the wake of Lennie Lawrence's departure. Chairman Roger Alwen said: "Although they lack managerial experience we feel they have the potential to make a successful team." Curbishley added: "We are delighted to be given this chance."

WEDNESDAY 25th JULY 2001

There were a few raised eyebrows among Charlton fans when the club paid £4m to acquire Tottenham defender Luke Young. But 'Youngy' proved to be one of Alan Curbishley's best buys and became one of the first names on the teamsheet during Charlton's Premiership stay. Chairman Richard Murray said: "Given that we are also spending £9m on The Valley's north stand, I feel that this latest transfer underlines the scale of our ambition."

FRIDAY 26th JULY 1963

At a board meeting on this day, a list of possible new nicknames for Charlton was discussed. It was eventually decided to drop the name 'Robins' in favour of either 'Crusaders' or 'Red Devils', as long as a suitable badge could be found. In the event, both proposed nicknames were scrapped and, in October, a new nickname of 'Valiants' was adopted.

WEDNESDAY 27th JULY 2005

Francis Jeffers and Jonatan Johansson both grabbed hat-tricks as a strong Charlton XI completely outclassed Aldershot Town. Jeffers finished with four goals and 'JJ' three as the Addicks ran out 8-0 winners.

WEDNESDAY 28th JULY 2010

Charlton chairman Richard Murray completed a share buy-out that saw him take full control of the club. "We will now go forward and actively seek new investment," he said. "This has been a critical time. Our future was uncertain and this was potentially one of our darkest hours."

SUNDAY 29th JULY 1951

Stuart Leary scored 126 of Charlton's 202-7 but still finished on the losing side as Kent County Cricket Club made 244-9 in an Arthur Fagg Benefit Match at Maidstone Athletic Ground. Charlton's star bowler was speed man Kevin Barry, a striker with the Addicks, who took four for 61.

MONDAY 30th JULY 2001

Charlton continued their preparations for the forthcoming Premiership season with a comfortable 5-1 victory against Swedish Second Division side Bodens. Richard Rufus, Jason Euell, Matt Svensson, Shaun Newton and Greg Shields supplied the goals in front of 5,000 fans.

MONDAY 31st JULY 2000

Less than a fortnight after buying Claus Jensen, Charlton splashed out again and completed the signing of Jonatan Johansson from Rangers for £3.75m. Boss Alan Curbishley said of the 24-year-old Finnish international: "He's quick, takes a goal well when he gets a chance, works hard and is at the age where we can affect him and he can affect us."

CHARLTON ATHLETIC
On This Day

AUGUST

WEDNESDAY 1st AUGUST 1979

The Derek Hales/Mike Flanagan saga finally reached some sort of closure on this day when the latter was transferred to Crystal Palace for the – then – huge fee of £650,000, a record deal between two London clubs. Flanagan, who had played no football for six months, said: "It's been a very frustrating time and I'm just looking forward to playing again."

THURSDAY 2nd AUGUST 1990

Relegation from the old First Division inevitably meant that some of Charlton's best players would be sold, so it was with sadness but no great surprise when fans heard that star striker Paul Williams had been transferred to Sheffield Wednesday. Williams, 24, was Charlton's top scorer in seasons 1988/89 and 1989/90 and was worth every penny of the £600,000 which The Owls paid for him.

TUESDAY 3rd AUGUST 1965

Frank 'Tiger' Hill was sacked as manager of Charlton on this day after nearly four years in the job. The club announced that Hill's contract, which had ended on 30th June, would not be renewed 'by mutual consent'. Chairman Michael Gliksten told the players after training, prompting John Hewie to say: "We had no inkling of it at all." Hill, 59, received a £625 pay-off.

THURSDAY 4th AUGUST 1976

Derek Hales didn't mind who he played against, as long as he could put the ball in the net. In the long hot summer of 1976, the somewhat unlikely opponents of East Arab Emirates arrived at Charlton's training ground and 'Killer' showed them no mercy, scoring four times in a 6-0 victory. Keith Peacock and Mike Flanagan completed the rout.

TUESDAY 5th AUGUST 2009

New signing Christian Dailly said he turned down several offers from Championship clubs to come to Charlton. The former Blackburn Rovers, West Ham United and Glasgow Rangers centre back, 35, impressed while on trial at The Valley and said: "There were a few offers from teams in the Championship but Charlton is perfect for me."

SATURDAY 6th AUGUST 1966

Identical twins Alan and Garry Kimble were born on this day. When they both appeared for Charlton on April 16th 1985, against Sheffield United at The Valley, they became only the third identical pair of twins to play in the Football League since the Second World War.

SATURDAY 7th AUGUST 1999

After the disappointment of relegation from the Premiership it was back to business as usual for Charlton – and Clive Mendonca – as the Addicks beat Barnsley 3-1. Mendonca grabbed a hat-trick, which included two penalties. But 'Super Clive' was still unhappy after missing a late chance. He said: "I've never scored four and I'll never get a better chance."

SATURDAY 8th AUGUST 1970

Perhaps no side came to The Valley with such an exotic name as The Accra Heart of Oak Sporting Club, from Ghana, who went down 3-1 to Charlton in today's close-season friendly.

SATURDAY 8th AUGUST 1998

A week before Charlton's first game in the Premiership, a testimonial took place between the Addicks and Hearts to mark Alan Curbishley's ten-year association with the club. On a scorching day, just 7,211 people turned up, which Curbs admitted had disappointed him. He added: "I had hoped West Ham would provide the opposition, which I think would have brought another 3,000 or 4,000 fans. I thought a game had been sorted out but, although it may seem hard to believe, Harry Redknapp and his assistant Frank Lampard forgot about the game."

WEDNESDAY 9th AUGUST 2000

Everybody associated with Charlton was distraught when 17-year-old Youth Academy member Pierre Bolangi drowned during a training exercise at Aldershot Barracks. Bolangi was a hugely popular boy with a massive beaming smile. An Army staff sergeant was later convicted of manslaughter after admitting failure to take adequate precautions to ensure the players' safety. A bust of Pierre was erected at the Sparrows Lane training ground in May 2007. Manager Alan Curbishley said: "In such a short period of time he managed to leave a lasting impression. When I think of him I remember that smile of his."

SATURDAY 10th AUGUST 1968

A second-minute goal by Keith Peacock was the first broadside fired in a classic derby against Millwall at The Valley which Charlton lost by the odd goal in seven. After Peacock's opener, The Lions hit back three times through Bryan Conlon, Derek Possee and Keith Weller. Ray Treacy pulled one back for the Addicks before Possee restored Millwall's two-goal advantage. Charlton piled forward and claimed a third 15 minutes from time through Harry Gregory, but it was Millwall who stole the points.

TUESDAY 10th AUGUST 2004

Charlton boss Alan Curbishley completed two major signings on this day in the shape of Danny Murphy and Francis Jeffers. Murphy cost £2.5m from Liverpool and Jeffers – known as the 'fox in the box' – cost £2.6m from Arsenal.

MONDAY 11th AUGUST 2003

Some transfers quicken the pulse and the news that mercurial Italian Paolo Di Canio had signed a one-year deal with Charlton did just that. The ex-West Ham United player said: "As soon as I met Alan Curbishley and Richard Murray I sensed this was a club with real ambition." Curbishley added: "I know he is going to be immensely popular with the club's fans."

TUESDAY 12th AUGUST 1980

Seventeen-year-old Paul Walsh became the youngest ever Charlton player to score a hat-trick as the Addicks sent Brentford tumbling out of the League Cup. 3-1 down after the first leg, Walsh and Charlton were brilliant in a 5-0 victory. Walsh said: "I took some stick last season because I wasn't getting into the right positions up front, but now I am concentrating on just that."

SATURDAY 13th AUGUST 2005

Two debut goals from Darren Bent gave Charlton their first opening day victory for five years with a 3-1 win at Sunderland. Bent – who came close to joining the Black Cats – scored after just 11 minutes and then clinched the points in injury time. Despite having Darren Ambrose sent off after 54 minutes, Charlton never looked in danger, and they also profited from a brilliant Danny Murphy free kick on 64.

TUESDAY 14th AUGUST 1945

Tommy Dowling, who died on this day aged 52, has a special place in the Charlton record books. He scored the club's first ever Football League goal in their inaugural league match, against Exeter City in August 1921.

SATURDAY 14th AUGUST 1971

Police made a number of ejections after fighting broke out behind one of the goals in the first game of the 1971/72 season against Hull City at The Valley. Charlton claimed the points thanks to a 72nd-minute goal from Ray Treacy.

TUESDAY 15th AUGUST 1989

Scot Joe McLaughlin became Charlton's record buy when Lennie Lawrence paid Chelsea £600,000 for his services. McLaughlin joined ex-Chelsea man Colin Pates, who signed the previous October. Lawrence said: "He had four successful seasons out of five with Pates at Chelsea."

SATURDAY 15th AUGUST 2009

Phil Parkinson insisted Charlton could make an immediate return to the Championship after seeing off Hartlepool United at Victoria Park. "We have to come to places like this and win if we are to achieve our aim of promotion this season," he said.

SATURDAY 16th AUGUST 1997

Barking-born Paul Konchesky became the youngest player to represent Charlton when he played against Oxford United at The Valley aged 16 years and 93 days. Konchesky performed admirably in the 3-2 win, prompting Alan Curbishley to say: "I never worried for a second about giving Paul his chance and he took it brilliantly."

TUESDAY 17th AUGUST 1971

When Theo Foley signed Watford's Barry Endean in February 1971, he thought he'd bought a proven goalscorer. Endean had scored 37 times in 93 appearances for the Hornets, but as soon as he pulled on a Charlton shirt he couldn't hit the proverbial bovine backside with a banjo. It wasn't until five months later – in his 19th match – that Barry finally opened his Addicks account in a 5-1 thrashing of Peterborough United in the first round of the League Cup.

SATURDAY 17th AUGUST 2002

Ten-man Charlton squandered a two-goal lead against Claudio Ranieri's Chelsea in an absorbing London derby at The Valley. The home crowd were ecstatic after just seven minutes when Paul Konchesky drilled home a fine, angled shot. But Konchesky went from hero to villain when he was controversially sent off after 26 minutes. Despite the disadvantage, Charlton went two ahead just after the half hour mark when Richard Rufus headed home. Chelsea gave themselves a lifeline when Gianfranco Zola pulled one back on 43. Charlton clung on vainly until six minutes from time, when Carlton Cole completed a splendid solo run by shooting past Dean Kiely. With just one minute remaining Frank Lampard grabbed a winner to break Charlton's hearts.

SUNDAY 18th AUGUST 1991

With the return to The Valley delayed yet again, footballing vagabonds Charlton crossed the Thames and briefly decamped to London E13 to set up home at Upton Park. Their first opponents on a baking hot day were Newcastle United. Robert Lee got the first goal and Carl Leaburn added a second to record a 2-1 victory for the Addicks in front of 9,320 fans.

TUESDAY 19th AUGUST 1969

With what one paper described as 'a sizzling display of headwork', striker Ray Crawford inspired a 3-2 victory over previously unbeaten Sheffield United. On 26 minutes, Crawford crowned a brilliant, sweeping five-man move, rising perfectly to head home a pinpoint cross from Keith Peacock. John Tudor equalised before Peacock himself made it 2-1 and then Crawford scored again with his head, diving courageously to beat Alan Hodgkinson. Gil Reece pulled one back for United, but the points stayed in SE7.

SATURDAY 19th AUGUST 2000

After an emotional and impeccably-observed one-minute silence for young Pierre Bolangi, whose family were in attendance, Charlton produced a fine performance in their first game back in the Premiership. Goals from Andy Hunt, John Robinson, Mark Kinsella and a Graham Stuart penalty gave Charlton a 4-0 win over Manchester City in front of 20,039 fans to put the Addicks at the Premiership summit, albeit briefly.

MARK KINSELLA CELEBRATES HIS GOAL DURING A 4-0 WIN OVER MANCHESTER CITY IN AUGUST 2000

MONDAY 20th AUGUST 1991

The return to The Valley saga hit another barrier on this day when Kier Construction group left the site in a row over money. It scuppered any prospect of Charlton returning home on the proposed date of 14th September 1991.

SATURDAY 21st AUGUST 1965

At eleven minutes past three, at Burnden Park, home of Bolton Wanderers, Charlton goalkeeper Mike Rose injured his right knee and could play no further part. It was the first day that the new substitute rule came into force and so, when Keith Peacock replaced Rose, both men put their names in the record books by becoming the first ever substitute and first player to be replaced in Football League history. The match was also Bob Stokoe's first in charge, ending in a 4-2 defeat for the Addicks.

SATURDAY 22nd AUGUST 1998

Charlton sat proudly at the top of the Premiership table after thrashing Southampton 5-0 at The Valley. It was the first time the Addicks had been in first place in the top tier since 1937/38. Striker Clive Mendonca grabbed the headlines with a hat-trick. After the game Mendonca said: "Can we stop the league now, please?"

TUESDAY 23rd AUGUST 1988

The body of the brilliant, multi-talented sportsman Stuart Leary was recovered from the slopes of Table Mountain in Cape Town, after he had been reported missing five days earlier. The subsequent verdict was suicide. Leary, who was arguably the greatest player ever to pull on the famous red shirt of Charlton, was just 55.

SATURDAY 23rd AUGUST 2003

There was a party atmosphere at Molineux as Wolverhampton Wanderers staged their first top-flight match there for 19 years. But Charlton gatecrashed it in spectacular style, winning 4-0 – their biggest Premiership win at an away venue. All four goals were scored in a first-half blitz which began when Jason Euell slotted home after just five minutes. Ten minutes later, Claus Jensen curled a brilliant free kick past Mike Oakes and then two more quick goals from Shaun Bartlett made the game safe.

SATURDAY 24th AUGUST 1957

In their first game back in the Second Division, a six-goal thriller at Huddersfield Town was merely an hors d'oeuvre for what would happen later in the season. Charlton raced into a three goal lead at Leeds Road courtesy of goals from Sam Lawrie, Stuart Leary and Johnny Summers, but fell apart after the interval as Town stormed back to make it 3-3. The return match at Charlton in December would go down as one of the greatest in Football League history.

SATURDAY 25th AUGUST 1951

Legendary Charlton manager Jimmy Seed knew a good player when he saw one, and was positively effusive in his praise of 23-year-old debutant John Hewie. In his match report of the 1-0 defeat at Portsmouth, Seed wrote: "Hewie ranks as one of the finest backs I've ever seen. He has everything, physical and mental, a great footballer needs." South African-born Hewie played 530 matches for Charlton, scoring 38 goals. By virtue of his Scottish father, Hewie also won 19 full caps for Scotland.

WEDNESDAY 25th AUGUST 2004

Two first-half goals in the space of five minutes by new signing Franny Jeffers put Charlton in the driving seat against David O'Leary's Aston Villa. Jeffers, a £2.6m summer capture from Arsenal, first planted a solid header past Thomas Sorensen following a Hermann Hreidarsson cross. Then he capitalised after Olof Mellberg spooned a clearance skywards and volleyed adroitly into the net. Villa, who emerged without Sorensen for the second half, were put out of sight when Luke Young applied the *coup de grace*, racing onto a Mark Fish pass and shooting under the body of the advancing substitute goalkeeper, Stefan Postma.

MONDAY 26th AUGUST 1963

Charlton's Young England centre-half Marvin Hinton moved across London to Chelsea on this day for £30,000. The Addicks accepted Chelsea's bid at noon on the Sunday, less than 24 hours after a 6-1 thrashing by Southampton at The Dell, but this did not stop Chelsea boss Tommy Docherty making his move for the highly-rated Croydon-born 23-year-old.

SATURDAY 26th AUGUST 2000

It's not often you score three goals at Arsenal and still lose, but that's what happened to Charlton on this day after an eight-goal thriller at Highbury. Charlton could not have played any better but, in the end, were undone by the sheer brilliance of Frenchmen Patrick Vieira and Thierry Henry. Vieira opened the scoring before two quick goals from Andy Hunt put Charlton ahead. Henry equalised after half-time before a fine finish from Graham Stuart made it 3-2 to Charlton. The imperious Vieira then took over and orchestrated a stunning second-half display by The Gunners which yielded three more goals and a 5-3 victory. But Charlton won praise for a fine attacking display, and Arsenal manager Arsène Wenger praised them as a much improved outfit who would easily avoid relegation.

SATURDAY 27th AUGUST 1921

Charlton played their first game as a league club on this day, beating Exeter City 1-0 in front of 13,000 spectators at The Valley. Tommy Dowling scored the winner after 33 minutes. A report in the *Daily Express* read: "Charlton deserved their victory but the team has yet to settle down. The forwards have not the necessary cohesion to win with regularity." But the reporter reserved special praise for Charlton's Dan Bailey, Sid Castle and, particularly, half-back Walker Hampson, who was described as 'brilliant'.

SATURDAY 27th AUGUST 1955

Stuart Leary marked his 100th league match with a brilliant hat-trick at Burnden Park, where Charlton beat Bolton Wanderers 3-1. The great South African scored in the 20th, 66th and 88th minutes to give Charlton their first win of the season following draws against Luton Town and Sheffield United. Nat Lofthouse grabbed a goal for The Trotters just before half-time.

SATURDAY 28th AUGUST 1920

Charlton Athletic made their professional debut on this day in the Southern League when they travelled to Norwich City and, in front of 1,000 spectators at a ground called The Nest, beat the Norfolk side 2-1 with goals from A Legge and Albert 'Mosky' Mills.

TUESDAY 28th AUGUST 1984

Derek Hales became Charlton's leading scorer in all competitions when he netted the Addicks' first goal in this 2-2 draw against Huddersfield Town at The Valley. 'Killer' equalled Stuart Leary's record of 163 goals when he bagged a hat-trick at Cardiff on the opening day of the season and then surpassed it with his 71st-minute goal against the Terriers.

SUNDAY 28th AUGUST 2005

'Addicks Love The New Denn' was how one tabloid newspaper headlined a report about Charlton's impressive 3-0 win at Middlesbrough in which Dennis Rommedahl played a leading role. The Danish winger used his electric pace to latch onto a Danny Murphy pass and fire home left-footed from the edge of the box seven minutes before the break. A rare Chris Perry goal made it two before Darren Bent capped a fine team display with a goal in the last minute.

TUESDAY 29th AUGUST 1972

Charlton really turned on the style against Swansea City at The Valley, but the game was watched by their lowest league gate for 40 years. A meagre 4,283 showed up to see midfielder Peter Reeves score a rare goal and open the floodgates for a 6-0 victory. Charlton, who lost Eamonn Rogers after just nine minutes, grew in confidence and went 3-0 up thanks to two goals from Arthur Horsfield. Midfielder Paul Davies pulled the strings. The man who replaced Rogers was on loan from Arsenal and was rewarded with a goal after 86 minutes. Dave Shipperley also helped himself to a brace to complete the rout.

TUESDAY 29th AUGUST 1989

Three brilliant goals saw Charlton send early First Division leaders Chelsea back to west London with their tails between their legs. In one of the best Charlton performances at Selhurst Park, the 'home' fans in the 17,221 crowd were treated to a vintage performance and a 3-0 win. The victory was crowned by a stunning left-foot shot from Paul Mortimer which cannoned in off the underside of the bar. Two classy strikes from Paul Williams had earlier put Charlton in the driving seat. Manager Lennie Lawrence said: "The finishing tonight was devastating. I can't recall a better goal than our third (Mortimer's) in my time at Charlton."

SATURDAY 29th AUGUST 1998

Charlton's first two games in the Premiership resulted in a 0-0 draw at Newcastle United and a 5-0 home win against Southampton. When Charlton secured another 0-0 draw against Arsenal at Highbury, it meant they had gone an incredible ten league matches without conceding a goal – one short of the national record.

SATURDAY 30th AUGUST 1986

Under-fire Manchester United boss Ron Atkinson admitted Charlton were the better side after the newly-promoted Addicks pulled off a sensational 1-0 win at Old Trafford. A 49th-minute goal from Mark Stuart was enough to clinch the points. Stuart said: "I saw my shot creep in and thought 'thank God for that'. I have never experienced anything like that before." After the match, Atkinson told reporters: "They were the better side and worked harder."

SATURDAY 31st AUGUST 1968

Charlton boss Eddie Firmani said his top-of-the-table side were 'too cocky' after throwing away a two-goal lead in a thriller against Crystal Palace at Selhurst Park. With just eight minutes gone, Charlton were two up through Ray Treacy and Matt Tees, but they allowed The Eagles to storm back and go 3-2 ahead. Harry Gregory then missed a penalty for the Addicks, but parity was restored three minutes later when Alan Campbell scored. A brilliant, attacking game was a great advert for the Second Division and meant Charlton remained at the top of the table after seven games.

CHARLTON ATHLETIC
On This Day

SEPTEMBER

SATURDAY 1st SEPTEMBER 1956

An 8-1 mauling for Charlton – their record defeat – at Sunderland signalled Jimmy Seed's final match as manager after more than 23 years. The team had made an appalling start to the season before the catastrophe at Roker Park with a performance marked by what one reporter described as "a paralysis of indecision". Seed's dismissal was the end of an era, though the way the club handled it was a disgrace.

SATURDAY 2nd SEPTEMBER 1972

A crazy 30 seconds settled a humdrum home game against York City. After 38 minutes, Charlton's Vinny O'Kane conceded a penalty for handball on the line. John Mackin stepped up, but saw his effort saved by John Dunn who released quickly and set up a new attack. The unfortunate Mackin hared back to defence and punched out an effort from Mike Flanagan. O'Kane, the original culprit, then stepped up and fired home the penalty.

WEDNESDAY 3rd SEPTEMBER 1947

Following the 1947 FA Cup Final victory, the following season Charlton started shipping goals at an alarming rate. After a 4-0 victory over Sheffield United they then conceded four against Arsenal and six at Manchester United. When they travelled to Highbury for the return match their plans were shattered when Peter Croker was injured after eight minutes. Arsenal went on to win 6-0, including four from the prolific Reg Lewis.

MONDAY 3rd SEPTEMBER 1956

One of the more shameful episodes in Charlton's history occurred today with the sacking of Jimmy Seed in a spineless, cowardly manner. Seed was summoned to meet chairman Stanley Gliksten and summarily dismissed. Except the press were spun a line that Seed had retired, and the following game's programme said he had resigned. It was an undignified end to the career of a man who had put Charlton on the footballing map. As reporter Desmond Hackett wrote: "Charlton Athletic without Jimmy Seed's beaming smile and throaty chuckle seems unthinkable."

SUNDAY 4th SEPTEMBER 1977

Furious Charlton boss Andy Nelson called his squad in for extra training after a 7-1 hammering at Luton Town. A pitiful display prompted him to order five extra sessions before the home game against Leyton Orient.

SATURDAY 5th SEPTEMBER 2009

After beating Brentford 2-0 at The Valley, Charlton registered their best ever start to any season, winning the first six matches. Early goals from Deon Burton and Lloyd Sam were enough to defeat the men from Griffin Park in front of the Sky TV cameras. It was also the sixth consecutive game that boss Phil Parkinson had named an unchanged starting line-up, equalling a record set at the beginning of season 1969/70.

SATURDAY 6th SEPTEMBER 1913

Charlton played their first game at the Angerstein Athletic Ground on Horn Lane, on the edge of the Greenwich Marshes and about a quarter of a mile from the River Thames. Their opponents, in the Southern Suburban League match, were Army Ordnance. Charlton won 3-1, watched by 500 spectators. Charlton shared the ground with Deptford Invicta and charged threepence admission for each game.

SATURDAY 6th SEPTEMBER 1969

Without a win or a goal in their last three games, Charlton lost star defender Paul Went for two months on this day. Went landed awkwardly in a home game against Cardiff City and needed a cartilage operation. Manager Eddie Firmani said he had a ready-made replacement for Went with John Keirs but was getting increasingly concerned about the side's lack of firepower. "Our failure to score is most disappointing," he added. *Daily Express* reporter Nigel Clarke claimed Firmani was looking at Ipswich Town's John O'Rourke, with the Portman Road club interested in taking Keith Peacock to Suffolk.

FRIDAY 7th SEPTEMBER 1934

Ten minutes after the arrival of his sister and mother at his bedside in a Torquay hospital, Charlton goalkeeper Alex Wright, 30, died from the injuries he received in a bathing accident at Torre Sands. Wright suffered a broken neck and fractured spine after diving off a raft into three feet of water and forcefully hitting his head on the sea bed. Charlton manager Jimmy Seed said: "Alex lived for his football and was a grand team man." Chairman Albert Gliksten added: "He was liked by everyone and had a brilliant career in front of him." Fifteen thousand people lined the three-mile route of his cortege at his funeral in his home town of Kilmarnock.

SATURDAY 7th SEPTEMBER 1985

Shock, anger, bemusement...all of these emotions and more were experienced by Charlton fans arriving for this day's home game against Crystal Palace. They were handed a hastily written sheet of paper informing them that the game would be the penultimate match ever played at The Valley and that, after the home match against Stoke on September 21st, the club would, with the richest of ironies, be based at Selhurst Park. The 3-1 victory over Palace was largely irrelevant as fans struggled to digest the bombshell. As an exercise in public relations and customer consultation it was laughable in its ineptitude.

SATURDAY 8th SEPTEMBER 1956

According to *Daily Express* reporter John Batson, the 'glowing, hypnotic eyes' of the absent, sacked Jimmy Seed seemed to be watching over Charlton as they fought back from 4-2 down to claim a draw against Sheffield Wednesday at The Valley. In the first match since the great man's sacking, Charlton drew after twice being two goals in arrears, inspired by what Batson described as Seed's 'strange eyes glittering, white mane bristling, as if he was pouring himself into his men on The Valley pitch.'

MONDAY 8th SEPTEMBER 1969

Chris Powell, who was born on this day, is one of the most popular players ever to play for the club, and his appointment as manager in January 2011 was greeted with genuine delight. Signed from Derby County in June 1998, Powell was so consistently good that Sven-Goran Eriksson picked him for England at the unusually late age of 31, making him the oldest England debutant for 47 years. Powell also served as chairman of the PFA and ended his playing career at Leicester before returning to The Valley following Phil Parkinson's sacking.

SATURDAY 9th SEPTEMBER 1967

"Now here's a happy fellow," said Charlton boss Bob Stokoe after Crystal Palace manager Bert Head put a consoling arm around him after a 3-0 win for the Glaziers at Selhurst Park. A few hours later, Stokoe may have needed more consoling after the Charlton board decided to dispense with his services. But happier days were ahead for the 36-year-old, who went on to lead Sunderland to stunning FA Cup success in 1973.

MONDAY 9th SEPTEMBER 1968

Clive Mendonca, who was born on this day, will forever be talked about in Charlton circles for his superlative hat-trick in the never-to-be-forgotten play-off final against Sunderland in May 1998. Mendonca, ironically, was born in Sunderland, and had two spells at Sheffield United, as well as stints with Doncaster Rovers and Rotherham United. He moved to Grimsby Town, from where Charlton bought him for £700,000 in the summer of 1997. In his first season for the Addicks, Mendonca scored 28 goals in all competitions and became the first Charlton player to score 20 league goals in a season since Mike Flanagan in 1976/77.

WEDNESDAY 10th SEPTEMBER 1958

When Sidcup-born striker Eddie Werge put Charlton 1-0 up after six minutes at Barnsley's home ground of Oakwell, it looked like the Addicks might be on course for their third win in a row. Wrong! After Werge's opener, Charlton crumpled and Barnsley – spearheaded by four goals from striker Malcolm Graham – went on to win the game 7-1.

FRIDAY 10th SEPTEMBER 1976

Another game at The Valley and another bagful of goals for Derek Hales. Hales plundered a headed hat-trick against Harry Haslam's Luton Town, scoring after 26, 37 and 60 minutes. Charlton eventually won 4-3, prompting manager Andy Nelson to say: "Derek doesn't miss much in front of goal but we still have plenty of work to do." Charlton's fourth came from a Bob Curtis penalty.

MONDAY 11th SEPTEMBER 1967

"This is the greatest day of my life – I still can't believe the news." Those were the words of Eddie Firmani after being appointed Charlton's new manager in the wake of Bob Stokoe's sacking. "I believe this club can become great again," he added. "I have always been devoted to Charlton because they are the club I owe almost everything to." Club chairman Michael Gliksten, who broke the news to the players, said: "Eddie has grown up with this club, knows the set-up and we think has the characteristics to become a good manager." Firmani's first match in charge was a 3-0 win at The Valley over Aston Villa.

WEDNESDAY 11th SEPTEMBER 1974

A small clump of Addicks fans who'd travelled north to watch Charlton's second-round Football League Cup tie against Manchester United were rewarded with a first-minute stunner from battling midfielder Peter Hunt. But then Charlton were quite simply steamrollered by a team still stinging from the humiliation of relegation from the First Division the previous April. Though United eventually won 5-1, Hunt's goal will always be remembered by those Addicks fans there to see it.

SATURDAY 12th SEPTEMBER 1953

Manager Jimmy Seed described Charlton's forward line as 'rampant and unstoppable' after the Addicks stormed to a record-breaking 8-1 home win against Middlesbrough. Despite Boro leading through a fifth-minute goal from Johnny Spuhler, Charlton delighted the 23,790 crowd with a feast of attacking football and eight goals, including a hat-trick from Eddie Firmani, two apiece for Sid O'Linn and Gordon Hurst and one for Stuart Leary. Charlton scored six times in the final 26 minutes of the match.

WEDNESDAY 12th SEPTEMBER 1956

After the distasteful and spineless sacking of Jimmy Seed, Charlton promoted trainer Jimmy Trotter to manager after nearly 23 years at the club. Chairman Stanley Gliksten said: "We are no longer looking for a manager. The directors met and decided to give the job to Jimmy Trotter and I don't think we could have made a better choice." Director David Clark explained the new Valley set-up rather obliquely as: "One Jimmy taking over from the other, except that Jimmy Trotter has been relieved entirely of office work."

SATURDAY 12th SEPTEMBER 1964

Referee Fred Schofield angered Charlton players after disallowing a late goal which would have given the Addicks a 5-4 win at Derby. The goal that got away came in the 86th minute, when Rams keeper Reg Matthews dropped a corner from his namesake Roy Matthews. Len Glover netted but Schofield blew for offside. On the train back to London, Eddie Firmani told reporter John Lloyd: "The referee made a mistake. I went up with the Derby keeper but we both missed the ball and it went straight to Glover who scored."

SATURDAY 13th SEPTEMBER 1919

The first ever game was played at The Valley on this day. It was an 'A' team fixture against Summerstown which Charlton won 2-0. At the end of their first season, Charlton won election from the Kent League to the Southern League.

SATURDAY 13th SEPTEMBER 1969

Monty Python first appeared on television in this year and one of its most famous sketches was 'The Spanish Inquisition', where a bemused old lady is 'tortured' with comfy cushions. And cushions were the weapons of choice in a bizarre confrontation between some Norwich City supporters and Charlton coach Theo Foley at the end of a controversial 1-1 draw at Carrow Road. City fans were furious at the end of a match littered with fouls and dissent and vented their spleen by hurling cushions at Foley who responded by hurling one back. Charlton chairman Michael Gliksten said: "I think the incident is best forgotten."

SATURDAY 14th SEPTEMBER 2002

Charlton boss Alan Curbishley empathised with the Addicks fans streaming away from The Valley after witnessing a footballing masterclass by Arsenal. "They will know that they have just seen a very, very good side," he said. The game finished 3-0 to Arsenal, who created a new record by scoring in 45 consecutive top-flight matches.

SATURDAY 15th SEPTEMBER 1990

A loyal band of 1,730 Charlton fans headed south to Brighton & Hove Albion's Goldstone Ground desperately hoping that the team could prevent an unwanted club record. If they lost it would mean ten consecutive league defeats. Despite taking the lead through Gordon Watson, Charlton could not hang on and eventually succumbed to a 3-2 defeat. It was the worst sequence of league results since the relegation season of 1956/57.

THURSDAY 16th SEPTEMBER 1948

Abingdon referee E Crook was knocked out when a shot struck him on the base of the skull during today's match between Chelsea and Charlton at Stamford Bridge. Mr Crook was poleaxed after being hit by a first-time shot from Chelsea's Roy Bentley after 30 minutes. Goals from Gordon Hurst and Benny Fenton helped Charlton to a 2-2 draw.

SATURDAY 16th SEPTEMBER 2000

Of all the players Alan Curbishley bought while Charlton manager, few can have repaid the fee as well as the excellent Dean Kiely. The brilliant keeper was snapped up from Bury and was consistently outstanding during Charlton's Premiership stay. In the 1-0 win over Tottenham Hotspur at The Valley on this day, Kiely pulled off three world-class saves – including one from a Les Ferdinand rocket which had to be seen to be believed. Kiely said: "This is my first chance of playing in the top flight and I am loving every minute of it."

SATURDAY 17th SEPTEMBER 1960

While virtually all 11,778 people in The Valley were aware that today's Second Division match against Luton Town had kicked off, it seems that the Hatters' right-back Seamus Dunne wasn't. With less than a minute gone, Dunne inexplicably picked the ball up in his penalty area, seemingly oblivious to the fact that the game had started. Sam Lawrie converted the penalty. Half a minute later, the unfortunate Dunne was caught horribly out of position and Johnny Summers ran through unchallenged to make it two. Two further goals from Dennis Edwards ensured a 4-1 win for Charlton.

FRIDAY 18th SEPTEMBER 1987

When Lennie Lawrence completed the signature of 24-year-old Andy Jones from Port Vale on this day, there was excitement and high expectations among Charlton fans. The Wrexham-born striker had been scoring goals for fun at Vale and had won international recognition with Wales. Charlton paid £350,000 for his services and he made his senior debut at Sheffield Wednesday on September 26th. In truth, Jones never quite fulfilled his potential, although his tally of 20 goals in 61 full appearances and 18 as substitute was not a bad return.

SATURDAY 18th SEPTEMBER 1999

After Charlton recorded their first win at Sheffield United in 42 years, boss Alan Curbishley said his players would be happy to have their places threatened by the club's new three-year twinning arrangement with Inter Milan. Yet Charlton played superbly at Bramall Lane with two goals from Andy Hunt ensuring a 2-1 win.

SATURDAY 19th SEPTEMBER 1998

Charlton were unlucky not to claim all three points in a six-goal thriller at Anfield. The Addicks led twice through goals from Richard Rufus and Clive Mendonca before Liverpool edged 3-2 ahead with a second goal from Robbie Fowler. But with seven minutes left on the clock, Charlton sub Steve Jones swivelled in the area and blasted a great equaliser past Brad Friedel to send the travelling Addicks fans – including Squeeze frontman Glenn Tilbrook – wild with delight. Jones's exuberant celebration, involving a lengthy slide towards a corner flag, caused onlookers to wince.

WEDNESDAY 20th SEPTEMBER 1961

Let there be light! Rather later than most clubs, Charlton finally erected floodlights at The Valley and they were switched on for the first time for the evening game against Rotherham United on this day. The four 120-foot high steel towers carried 24 floodlight units, each having a 1,500-watt lamp. Alas, the illuminations brought no change in fortune to Charlton's poor start to the season and the Millers headed back to south Yorkshire with the points after a comfortable 2-0 win.

SATURDAY 21st SEPTEMBER 1985

There had been a mix of confusion and stunned disbelief when Charlton fans were handed that rather pathetic slip of paper containing such devastating news before the Crystal Palace game. On this day, the terrible reality dawned. Charlton were leaving their beloved Valley, seemingly never to return. The match against Stoke City was a mere bagatelle in terms of the greater issue – namely that The Valley's 66-year life as the home of Charlton Athletic was, apparently, coming to an end. Rancour, gloom and, perhaps most of all, bemusement, were the overriding emotions on that bleak day when Charlton, it seemed, bade farewell to a remarkable football ground and their home. In *Battle for The Valley*, Rick Everitt wrote that the groundshare was destined to fail because "Charlton Athletic and The Valley were one and the same thing. It was playing in Floyd Road, SE7, that gave the club its identity and the team its legitimacy in the eyes of the supporters. Take that away and eventually you would have nothing but a gang of mercenaries in red shirts."

SATURDAY 22nd SEPTEMBER 1906

The newly-formed Charlton Athletic club played its first ever competitive match on this day, travelling a few miles west to take on Nunhead Swifts Reserves in the Lewisham League. This historic match ended in a 6-1 victory for Charlton. It was the start of a highly successful season in which Charlton won 17 and drew one of their 18 matches and topped the league with 35 points.

TUESDAY 22nd SEPTEMBER 1992

Fans' favourite Robert Lee played some of the best football of his career during Charlton's 18-month spell at Upton Park, and it was inevitable that a big move would soon follow. On this day, Lee was unveiled as a Newcastle United player after Toon boss Kevin Keegan paid £700,000 for his services. Lee said the 'pull' of Newcastle was overwhelming and that Keegan had been his boyhood idol.

TUESDAY 23rd SEPTEMBER 1986

After experiencing the dismal, almost funereal atmosphere of Selhurst Park during a Littlewoods Cup tie against Lincoln City, which attracted a pitiful 2,319 onlookers, local journalist Peter Cordwell decided to take up the cudgels. In his match report in the *South East London Mercury*, Cordwell wrote: "Only an emperor with a penchant for parading around starkers would fail to see that Charlton have no real future at Selhurst Park. It can't go on like this." Cordwell's words were timely and much-needed. Something was stirring.

SATURDAY 23rd SEPTEMBER 1995

For several seasons from the late 1980s to the mid-1990s, 6ft 3in Lewisham-born striker Carl Leaburn divided opinion among many fans, with his goals-to-games ratio at the start of his career being less than impressive. Love him or loathe him, no-one could fault the big man's effort and commitment to the cause and the deep, slow, almost primeval chant of 'Lea-burn, Lea-burn' was increasingly heard at The Valley as the big man gradually won most of his doubters over. Perhaps his greatest day in a Charlton shirt came in the game on this day at Ipswich Town, when he scored a hat-trick in an incredible 5-1 win for the Addicks.

FRIDAY 24th SEPTEMBER 1976

Most neutrals were delighted when Southampton beat Manchester United to lift the FA Cup in May 1976, but just five months later they came to The Valley and were on the wrong end of a 6-2 hiding. Two goals apiece for Mike Flanagan and Derek Hales and one each for Paddy Powell and Richie Bowman sent the Saints back to Hampshire with red faces. Charlton boss Andy Nelson described it as the best performance he'd seen since taking over in 1974.

WEDNESDAY 25th SEPTEMBER 1963

Charlton frequently come unstuck in the north-west, and tonight's second-round League Cup game at Blackpool was business as usual. Despite getting off to a flier with Jack Kennedy's first-minute opener, Charlton were then overwhelmed by a Tangerine tsunami. The men from Bloomfield Road – who included Jimmy Armfield and Alan Ball in their line-up – proceeded to put seven goals past Charlton, including four for striker Ray Charnley.

SATURDAY 26th SEPTEMBER 1953

"There!" shouted 20-year-old Charlton centre-forward Stuart Leary to his inside-right Sid O'Linn, pointing imperatively to an open space on the left wing. O'Linn dutifully obeyed, the ball swung over and John Evans nodded in his second goal of the game. In the stand, Charlton manager Jimmy Seed was chuckling: "A case of the idol being told what to do by his admirer." Back in South Africa, Leary idolised the older O'Linn. The day belonged to Leary, who scored four goals in yet another brilliant Charlton display. Only two weeks after annihilating Middlesbrough, they beat Liverpool 6-0. Seed had this to say about Leary: "He's the cleverest, cleanest, most club-conscious centre-forward in the business."

WEDNESDAY 26th SEPTEMBER 1962

Second Division Charlton stunned top-flight Leicester City with an amazing four-goal comeback at Filbert Street in the League Cup. Hundreds of City fans left at half-time thinking their team's 4-0 lead had guaranteed them a fourth-round place. But Charlton had other ideas. A goal shortly after the break from Brian Kinsey began a fine comeback. Keith Peacock scored two goals and then, six minutes from time, Fred Lucas hammered home an unlikely equaliser.

SATURDAY 27th SEPTEMBER 1952

Just a quiet day at the seaside for Charlton, with four goals scored and a mere eight conceded! Yes, the records tumbled at Bloomfield Road when Charlton went down 8-4 to Blackpool. An own goal from Charlton's 'Squib' Hammond opened the floodgates in the sixth-minute and then the goals just kept going in. Twelve goals was the most scored in a First Division match at Bloomfield Road and it was also the first time Charlton had conceded more than seven goals in league or cup football.

SUNDAY 28th SEPTEMBER 2003

On his day, Charlton striker Kevin Lisbie could terrorise the very best defenders in the game. Yet his inconsistency and all too frequent failure to convert good chances alienated sections of The Valley crowd. It all came right for the Hackney-born 24-year-old, who grabbed a scintillating hat-trick on this day as Charlton beat Liverpool 3-2 in front of the Sky TV cameras.

SATURDAY 29th SEPTEMBER 1962

Somehow things were far more innocent yesteryear, weren't they? When a group of Charlton fans invaded The Valley pitch after a 3-2 defeat to Rotherham United, one of them made a beeline for referee H Horner with the aim of throwing a missile. But the choice of weapon was more slapstick than malicious, as the supporter splattered the unfortunate official with a large dollop of ice cream. Nevertheless, Mr 'Whippy' Horner was unamused and saw fit to make an official complaint in his match report.

SATURDAY 29th SEPTEMBER 2001

Fans arriving for today's Premiership match against Leicester City at The Valley found a new merchandising catalogue placed on every seat. Who could have foreseen that these would provide ammunition for a bizarre protest, quite unlike anything seen at The Valley before or since? On 26 minutes, popular Addicks defender Steve Brown was stretchered off after injuring his ankle, but referee Mike Dean also showed him a red card, claiming Brown had deliberately handled the ball. The Charlton fans were apoplectic and hundreds of the marketing catalogues rained down on to the pitch in protest. The incident appeared to galvanise the team, who went on to win the game 2-0 after City also had a player sent off.

SATURDAY 30th SEPTEMBER 2000

Charlton fans were confused when popular striker Andy Hunt was substituted immediately after scoring against Coventry City at The Valley. There was, however, a very good reason. It transpired Hunt was suffering from a condition called myalgic encephalitis (ME) or post-viral fatigue syndrome. Hunt had been feeling run down, lethargic and exhausted for some time, and eventually succumbed to the debilitating illness which ended his fine career. Hunt told author Charlie Connelly: "Apart from losing a leg, I can't think of anything worse for a professional footballer. It was just horrible." 'Hunty' finally announced his retirement in May 2001 and then proved he was far more imaginative and intrepid than the average footballer by relocating to Belize with his family and establishing an adventure travel company.

CHARLTON ATHLETIC
On This Day

OCTOBER

SATURDAY 1st OCTOBER 1960

Johnny Summers will always be remembered for that superlative, 'Boy's Own' performance when he scored five against Huddersfield Town in December 1957. However, he repeated the feat three seasons later when he bagged five against Portsmouth in a 7-4 Valley victory for Charlton. Summers was cheered off the pitch and, ten minutes after the final whistle, the sparse crowd of 10,692 were demanding his reappearance. Modest Summers said later: "The marking was really loose. Every time I hit the ball it seemed to go right. It was just my lucky day." It was left to manager Jimmy Trotter to do Summers justice: "Johnny is a great player and can hit the ball with either foot. Each goal was a gem." The other goals came from Eddie Werge and John Sewell.

SATURDAY 1st OCTOBER 1983

Brighton & Hove Albion manager Jimmy Melia said he felt sorry for Charlton after the Addicks were on the wrong end of a 7-0 pummelling at the Goldstone Ground. Charlton went into the game unbeaten in Division Two and there were even whispers about promotion, but they came spectacularly unstuck as goals rained in past Nicky Johns. Albion were 5-0 up at half-time and, with almost half an hour to go, had scored seven, including the first hat-trick of Jimmy Case's career. After the game, Melia told reporters: "On that form we would have beaten any team in the First Division, let alone the Second. I genuinely felt sorry for Charlton."

SATURDAY 1st OCTOBER 1988

The Charlton fans who made the journey to East Anglia for this First Division match against Norwich City were rewarded with a fine display from the Addicks. Despite falling behind to a 16th-minute goal from Andy Linighan, Charlton stormed back and equalised through Paul Williams after 37 minutes. With a small but vocal knot of Addicks fans roaring the team on in the autumnal sunshine, Charlton played wonderfully in the second half. First Paul Mortimer scored one of his classics – a typically mazy run, which took him past three defenders, before placing the ball past Bryan Gunn. Then, after 67 minutes, Williams grabbed his second to complete an excellent 3-1 victory.

MONDAY 2nd OCTOBER 1961

After a disastrous start to the season with eight defeats and just one win in the first 11 games, manager Jimmy Trotter was axed. The final straw for the directors was a 4-0 defeat at The Valley at the hands of Liverpool. However, with their usual 'Stalinist' desire to gloss over unpalatable news, Trotter – like Jimmy Seed before him – was said by Charlton to have resigned. Charlton historian Colin Cameron says: "Fans expecting to find a tribute in the next programme were to be disappointed because the only action Charlton took was to delete his name as manager." Quite why Charlton adopted this revisionist stance is unclear, but it would have been perfectly at home in George Orwell's *1984*.

THURSDAY 2nd OCTOBER 1969

After he refused to attend a special training session at Bisham Abbey, Charlton sacked striker Ray Crawford for breach of contract. Crawford had a blazing row with manager Eddie Firmani after claiming he was not given enough time to prepare for the trip, saying that his wife got nervous if left on her own. Firmani said: "I have taken disciplinary action against Crawford because he has broken his contract." Crawford hit back, saying: "I am contacting the PFA and if they cannot help me I will take legal action. I suppose this has been boiling up. I have nothing against Eddie but my style is not his style and this has led to a clash of personalities."

THURSDAY 2nd OCTOBER 1986

The entire back page of the *South East London Mercury* was devoted to a petition under the heading 'Our Home is The Valley'. Inside, another article was headed: 'Who cares and how much?' Fans were asked to sign the form and return it if they felt Charlton should leave Selhurst Park and return to The Valley. The response was astonishing. In the coming weeks, 15,000 people had signed and returned the forms. As Rick Everitt wrote in the excellent *Battle for The Valley*: "Easily the biggest postbag in the *Mercury*'s 153-year history, it amounted to an extraordinary sociological phenomenon, as if some great psychological dam which had been holding back this torrent of emotion had suddenly been opened."

TUESDAY 3rd OCTOBER 1995

A two-legged League Cup tie against Premiership Wimbledon finally went Charlton's way with an extra-time winner from John Robinson. Charlton had edged the thrilling first leg at Selhurst Park 5-4, with Lee Bowyer scoring a hat-trick. In the return leg at The Valley, the Dons won 3-2 in normal time, giving an aggregate score of 7-7. But Robinson's finish after 97 minutes finally settled the tie. Alan Curbishley said: "Tonight was a fantastic achievement for my young side – seven of them home grown."

SATURDAY 4th OCTOBER 1969

Cynics might well say there's been the occasional clown connected with Charlton down the years, but new forward-thinking marketing consultant Rodney Stone – a decent man with some good ideas – brought an even greater sense of the circus to The Valley before this league game with Portsmouth. First of all, Stone organised a spectacular display by the Surbiton-based Avondale Gymnastic Club. Then, even more bizarrely, a bemused-looking camel and baby elephant named Lulu paraded around the pitch. The fun and games continued in the first half with both teams scoring twice in this 2-2 draw.

SATURDAY 5th OCTOBER 1985

The horrible reality that The Valley was no longer Charlton's ground was brought home on this day when the team played its first 'home' match at Selhurst Park. Charlton laid on 12 double-decker buses to help fans make the 13-mile journey to London SE25. The team's fine start to the season continued with a 2-1 win over Sunderland. 5,552 fans watched, prompting manager Lennie Lawrence to announce pragmatically: "I doubt we'd have got many more at The Valley."

THURSDAY 6th OCTOBER 1988

Paul Miller was bought from Spurs in February 1987 in an attempt to bolster Charlton's defence and stave off relegation from Division One. Miller brought much-needed experience but his spell at Charlton ended in disgrace. On September 24th 1988 he was sent off for allegedly spitting at Andy Thorn during a game against Newcastle United at Selhurst Park. From that point on, Miller's card was marked and the ex-Spurs man never played for Charlton again. Miller, who made 52 appearances for Charlton, was transferred to Watford on this day for £85,000.

LEE BOWYER SCORED A HAT-TRICK AGAINST WIMBLEDON IN OCTOBER 1995

TUESDAY 7th OCTOBER 1975

A wonderful Charlton display deserved more than a 1-1 draw against an outstanding Queens Park Rangers side in this League Cup third-round tie at Loftus Road. The QPR side contained Stan Bowles, Gerry Francis and Dave Thomas and were one of the top three sides in the country at the time. Yet Charlton, smarting from a 5-0 reverse at Bolton the previous Saturday, were simply brilliant and snatched the lead when Colin Powell fired home after a sublime one-two with Mike Flanagan. Stan Bowles equalised on 68 minutes but manager Andy Nelson was a happy man and said: "I knew after the result at Bolton, the players were prepared to run themselves into the ground."

SATURDAY 8th OCTOBER 1938

Fleet Street scribe Desmond Hackett said that Charlton gave Manchester United such a footballing masterclass on this day that he felt sorry for the Old Trafford fans. Goals from George Green and 'Sailor' Brown gave Charlton a 2-0 victory prompting Hackett to eulogise about Charlton's 'full-powered raiding', 'mastery of the higher arts of soccer' and 'brainy, high-speed attacking'. "The goals in this game came through sheer Charlton ability," said Hackett.

SATURDAY 9th OCTOBER 1976

Derek Hales scored one of the finest goals ever seen at The Valley on this day. 'Killer' finished off a remarkable piece of wing play by Colin 'Paddy' Powell by firing an unstoppable left-footed volley past Hull City keeper Jeff Wealands as Charlton beat the Tigers 3-1. It was Hales's second goal in yet another hat-trick for the lethal marksman and was so good that it won ITV's Goal of the Season award. Hales received his award on 8th of May 1977 on *The Big Match*, with Colin Powell also in the studio.

FRIDAY 10th OCTOBER 2008

Charlton confirmed they had received an 'indicative cash offer' to buy the club from Dubai-based company Zabeel Investments. In a statement, the club said: "Should the offer be made formally to shareholders, the board would recommend shareholders to accept it. There is, however, no certainty that a formal offer will be made."

SATURDAY 11th OCTOBER 1986

A highlight of Charlton's first season back in the top flight was a 3-2 win over eventual champions Everton, with a hat-trick from Jim Melrose. The Scot scored after 20, 35 and 78 minutes to secure a great win against the men from Goodison Park, who were league champions in 1984/85 and runners-up in 1985/86. However, manager Lennie Lawrence, while delighted at the result, scoffed at the attendance of 10,564 against one of the country's top sides and called on Charlton fans to visit Selhurst Park in greater numbers.

TUESDAY 12th OCTOBER 1993

In the autumn of 1993, Charlton fans got a rare chance to see the team play a competitive match in Europe in the Anglo-Italian Cup. They lost 2-0 to Brescia, and then drew 1-1 with Ancona on the 9th of November, with Carl Leaburn scoring the goal. Boss Alan Curbishley said: "It was a good experience for our team and the fans but in many ways I could have done without the whole thing. There was no doubt that the extra games and travelling involved were disruptive."

SATURDAY 13th OCTOBER 1962

Charlton rode their luck and came back from Norwich City with a 4-1 victory. Reporter Don Woodward said the Canaries enjoyed 80 per cent of possession but could not convert their chances. Conversely, every time Charlton attacked they scored; goals coming from Brian Kinsey, two from Roy Matthews and a fourth from Dennis Edwards. Woodward said: "Honestly, the brightest thing about Charlton was their new shirts – white with black shoulders, a new change strip – but after some of the wretched luck they have had recently I cannot begrudge them a single cheer."

WEDNESDAY 14th OCTOBER 1970

Charlton manager Theo Foley could be forgiven for wondering whether he was coming or going following a hectic day of transfer activity at The Valley which saw talented Scottish midfielder Alan Campbell sold to Birmingham City for £70,000 and Gordon Riddick and Harry Gregory sold to Leyton Orient and Aston Villa respectively for £7,000. German-born defender Dietmar Bruck also arrived from Coventry City for £11,100.

SATURDAY 14th OCTOBER 1978

Charlton boss Andy Nelson considered today's 3-0 win at Leicester City the best away performance he'd seen in his four years as manager. Star of the show was Mike Flanagan, who scored twice and recaptured the form that won him an England B cap. Right-back Peter Shaw made Flanagan's first and then Martin Robinson chipped from the byline for Terry Brisley to nod home. Flanagan's second was a gem – he danced past City's right-back Steve Whitworth and then finished past Mark Wallington to leave most of the 14,277 Filbert Street crowd dumbstruck.

SATURDAY 15th OCTOBER 1977

Charlton striker Mike Flanagan came back to haunt Tottenham Hotspur – the club who let him go – with a sensational 11-minute hat-trick at The Valley as the Addicks thrashed Spurs 4-1. Watched by a bumper crowd of 30,706, Charlton took the lead after just two minutes through Hugh McAuley, only to be pegged back on 25 when Peter Taylor equalised. On 71 minutes, Flanagan began his three-goal blitz. He said afterwards: "I did not have a chance for 70 minutes and then had three in 11 minutes." Flanagan was with Spurs from the age of 11 to 18 and helped to win the Youth Cup in 1970 in a side that contained Steve Perryman and Barry Daines. There was also trouble in the covered end in the first half and referee Homewood had to briefly suspend play when some fans spilled on to the pitch to escape the fighting behind them. A number of fans were treated for minor injuries.

SATURDAY 16th OCTOBER 1976

After a thrilling 4-4 draw at Burnley – during which Charlton contrived to squander a 4-1 lead – vandals smashed the back window of the Addicks' team coach and a replacement had to be sent for. Master goal-taker Derek Hales scored twice, Bob Curtis converted a penalty after just two minutes and Mike Flanagan put Charlton 4-1 up, but the men from Turf Moor stormed back and levelled with three goals in 13 minutes through Peter Noble, Paul Fletcher and Terry Cochrane. Reporter Ronald Kennedy said: "Finishes like this are calculated to send even the coolest fan reaching for their bottle of nerve pills."

SATURDAY 17th OCTOBER 1964

Southampton's Terry Paine was inexcusably struck on the side of his head by a stone thrown from the East Terrace. Paine had incurred Charlton's wrath with a 37th-minute piece of gamesmanship when he jumped at the 'wrong' time as a cross came over. "I did it to put the Charlton defence off," said Paine. "He jumped into Brian Kinsey's back and stopped him clearing," countered Addicks skipper Mike Bailey. When the ball rolled loose, Paine stuck it past Charlton keeper Ken Jones. Shortly after Paine was hit by a missile near the East Terrace: "It felt like a stone and hit me on the side of the head," said Paine. Goals from Lenny Glover and Keith Peacock were not enough to save Charlton from a 5-2 trouncing.

MONDAY 18th OCTOBER 1982

Many people thought it was a joke or a publicity stunt when it was announced that twice former European Player of the Year Allan Simonsen was set to join Charlton from Spanish giants Barcelona. When the news leaked out on September 8th, there was general disbelief throughout the game and, during the course of a protracted saga, even the most diehard Charlton fan was convinced it would not happen. But, incredibly, the 29-year-old Dane put pen to paper on this day to become a Charlton player in a deal eventually valued at £324,000. He only made 17 appearances for the club but, in that time, Simonsen scored nine goals and was clearly head-and-shoulders above both his team-mates and his opponents.

SATURDAY 19th OCTOBER 1985

Less than a month after Charlton left The Valley, two-goal Alan Curbishley voiced the club's new-found optimism for promotion after a 5-3 win at fellow promotion hopefuls Brighton & Hove Albion pushed them into third place. After the impressive Goldstone Ground win, Curbishley said: "There is still a long way to go but we have got to have a very good chance now because we have played most of the top teams away from home now. Most of them have got to come to 'our' ground in the last few weeks of the season and that must favour us." George Shipley, Robert Lee and Mike Flanagan were Charlton's other scorers.

MONDAY 20th OCTOBER 1986

If you could point to one event when the return to The Valley campaign really gathered pace, it was the supporters' club AGM held on this day. "We'll be there!" screamed the back page of the *Mercury* on October 16th, encouraging fans to attend en masse. And attend they did – The Valley Club could cope with 400 people, but there were at least 1,000 on that autumnal evening when the voices of disgruntled fans started to be heard. The supporters' club officials were unhappy that their AGM had been hijacked. The irony, of course, was that the very people whose presence angered the effete supporters' club were precisely those supporters who they should have been representing all along.

SATURDAY 21st OCTOBER 1972

Oldham Athletic were furious after a Peter Hunt shot which hit the side-netting in the 82nd minute was given as a goal. Referee Powell awarded it, putting the Addicks 4-2 up. As the Latics party boarded their coach back to Lancashire, one of their directors stormed: "The fourth goal did not go in the net and we were given two indirect free kicks when the verdict was a penalty or nothing."

SATURDAY 22nd OCTOBER 1960

Charlton secretary Jack Phillips claimed 50 young Addicks fans cost the team victory after an amazing 6-6 draw with Middlesbrough at The Valley. With 90 seconds left, Johnny Summers equalised with an angled shot from 30 yards. Yelling with delight, the boys swarmed across the pitch dancing with joy. But Phillips said: "In the time it took to clear the pitch, we might well have had another goal." That was certainly a possibility in this astonishing thriller containing seven goals in a 17-minute spell. There were stunning individual performances from Charlton's Dennis Edwards and Boro's Brian Clough, who both scored hat-tricks, and the Teesiders' pint-sized keeper Bob Appleby also pulled off four dazzling saves.

THURSDAY 23rd OCTOBER 2008

Dubai-based consortium Zabeel Investments confirmed they would not be buying Charlton. A statement from the club said the consortium had decided to focus on domestic opportunities instead. Manager Alan Pardew said: "With the credit crisis the deal was always in danger."

SATURDAY 23rd OCTOBER 2010

Striker Paul Benson grabbed a dramatic late winner after Charlton looked to have squandered a 3-0 lead at Carlisle United. After 47 minutes, the Addicks were 3-0 ahead courtesy of goals from Johnnie Jackson, Joe Anyinsah and Benson. But the Cumbrians hit back with three goals of their own inside 19 minutes. Then, with the game in stoppage time, the Addicks won a corner. Simon Francis fired it in and Benson rose to head the ball firmly in to the net, sparking delirium among the 313 Addicks' fans who had made the long journey north.

TUESDAY 24th OCTOBER 2001

As Charlton took to the field for tonight's Premiership match at Villa Park, one player stood out and another was conspicuous by his absence. Goalkeeper Dean Kiely was sporting a spectacular shiner and there was no sign of defender Andy Todd. Alan Curbishley revealed all in his press conference after the 1-0 defeat – Kiely and Todd had clashed during training and, later, Todd approached Kiely and struck him hard in the face. Curbs was furious and, after leaving Todd behind while the squad travelled to Birmingham, decided he would also have to let him go. Todd's Charlton career was over.

SATURDAY 25th OCTOBER 1986

Jim Melrose scored the fastest goal in Charlton's history against West Ham United at Upton Park. The Hammers kicked off and the ball was played to Tony Gale, who gave it straight to Robert Lee. Lee played in Melrose, who tucked the ball past West Ham keeper Phil Parkes. Just nine seconds had elapsed. The eventual 3-1 win meant it was five wins on the trot for the Addicks.

WEDNESDAY 26th OCTOBER 2005

Following a dramatic penalty shoot-out at Stamford Bridge, Charlton dumped Jose Mourinho's Chelsea out of the Carling Cup. It was the first time in 37 matches and 15 months that Chelsea had tasted defeat at home. After John Terry put the Blues ahead, Darren Bent capitalised on a Robert Huth error to equalise. In a dramatic penalty shoot-out, it was left to Bryan Hughes to hold his nerve and score past Carlo Cudicini to give Charlton a memorable 5-4 win on penalties.

SATURDAY 27th OCTOBER 1956

Eighteen-year-old Brian Kinsey was a disappointed young man as he left the dressing room following today's 1-1 draw against Newcastle. He told reporter Norman Dixon: "I know I didn't have a good game, I was too tense." Hard to believe that the callow-sounding, Charlton-born teenager would go on to enjoy such a fine career for the club. He was an automatic first choice throughout the entire 1960s and, by the time he moved to South Africa in 1971, had made 418 first-team outings, scoring 26 goals.

SATURDAY 27th OCTOBER 2001

The upper tier of The Valley's £9m North Stand extension was partially opened for the first time on this day, resulting in a record attendance since the return home in 1992. Unfortunately, most of the 22,658 spectators – who included England boss Sven-Goran Eriksson – went home disappointed after Liverpool won 2-0.

SATURDAY 28th OCTOBER 1933

Daily Express reporter Trevor Wignall made a special visit to The Valley to see for himself 'what all the fuss is about'. Wignall said: "This club in a suburb of London has contrived to push even the Arsenal into the background, and if that is not a feat worthy of mention I would much like to know what is." Charlton's opponents were Torquay United and Wignall noted the number of scouts and managers from other clubs watching the match. Charlton did not disappoint, putting six goals past the Devonians without reply. Wignall finished his report with impressive prescience: "A phrase I used last week – 'look out for Charlton' – is worth repeating again."

TUESDAY 28th OCTOBER 1986

Nothing could stop Charlton in the early autumn of 1986, although the Selhurst Park floodlights very nearly did. After 69 minutes of this League Cup third-round tie against Queens Park Rangers – with Charlton leading 1-0 – the lights failed, delaying the game for 20 minutes. Charlton's goal was scored by Steve Thompson, his first in 55 games for the club. Manager Lennie Lawrence said: "It's a good job the game could be completed because we'd never have heard the end of it from 'Thommo' otherwise. He's waited a long time for that one."

THE UPPER TIER OF CHARLTON'S NEW NORTH STAND OPEN FOR THE FIRST TIME IN OCTOBER 2001

SATURDAY 29th OCTOBER 1955

Some vintage left-wing triangle play between Billy Kiernan, Ron White and 'Squib' Hammond was the catalyst for a brilliant 4-2 win for Charlton against Arsenal at Highbury. According to reporter Bob Pennington, Charlton were so dominant that they were unlucky not to score six in a second-half blitz. The goals came from 'Buck' Ryan, Kiernan, White and Stuart Leary in front of a crowd of 47,138.

SATURDAY 30th OCTOBER 1948

"This is the best football I've seen Charlton play in years," said reporter Frank Butler after watching the Addicks trounce Sunderland 4-0 at The Valley. Goals from Charlie Vaughan and Gordon Hurst inside the first 11 minutes put Charlton on their way, and second-half goals from South African Sid O'Linn and Benny Fenton completed the rout. Butler praised the performances of Fenton and Charlie Revell and commented that O'Linn's £250 boat fare compared favourably with the £20,050 Sunderland paid for Len Shackleton.

FRIDAY 31st OCTOBER 1975

Ahead of Charlton's 2,000th Football League match, Derek Hales promised he would take advantage of what he saw as deficiencies in Southampton's back line. Perhaps only Killer could make such a bold statement and then live up to it as well. Hales struck twice, after 13 and 68 minutes, in a 4-1 win for Charlton with Peter Osgood grabbing a late consolation for the Saints.

CHARLTON ATHLETIC
On This Day

NOVEMBER

SATURDAY 1st NOVEMBER 1980

The champagne corks were popping after Charlton created a new club record on this day with their seventh successive win. It took a fluke headed goal from Phil Walker to beat Huddersfield Town, who had previously not lost at their Leeds Road ground for 11 months. But, Mike Bailey's side were on a run of unstoppable form and he forked out £24 for the celebratory bubbly. Charlton did not lose until Boxing Day when they went down 1-0 at Oxford United – a run of 15 games without defeat.

TUESDAY 2nd NOVEMBER 2010

A low drive from midfielder Johnnie Jackson resulted in a history-making 5,000th league goal for Charlton. Jackson's 13th-minute strike was the opener in an impressive 3-0 victory over Swindon Town at the County Ground. It was the Addicks' third successive league victory. A superb back header by Joe Anyinsah, and a more prosaic effort by Paul Benson, completed the victory.

TUESDAY 3rd NOVEMBER 1998

At a ceremony held at the Barbican Centre in London, manager Alan Curbishley was awarded an honorary Masters degree by Greenwich University, whose spokeswoman Karen Jones said: "Every year we award a small number of honorary degrees which are awarded to people who are particularly distinguished in their field."

SUNDAY 4th NOVEMBER 2001

When Thierry Henry put Arsenal ahead after six minutes it looked like being a very long afternoon for black-shirted Charlton. What happened next though was the stuff of dreams. Despite being outplayed, Charlton went into the break 2-1 up thanks to goals from Steve Brown, and a Richard Wright own goal. The second half was a different story and, on 49 minutes, to the joy of the travelling fans, a sublime chip from Claus Jensen made it 3-1. When Jason Euell made it four, a few minutes later, the Addicks fans were pinching themselves. Henry's penalty on the hour made it 4-2 but this was one of the most remarkable and memorable Charlton performances for a long time and was preserved for posterity with a special, cleverly-titled video called 'Black Sabbath'. It was Charlton's first victory at Highbury since October 1956 and equalled the most number of goals Arsenal had conceded there in the Premiership.

SATURDAY 5th NOVEMBER 1955

Charlton manager Jimmy Seed was presented with a problem all managers would like after 'Buck' Ryan scored four times in a 5-2 demolition of Manchester City at The Valley. With Charlton scoring 15 times in the last three matches, Seed could find no place in the starting line-up for strikers Bobby Ayre and Jimmy Gauld. But the canny Seed, a master of man-management, smiled: "Both are decent fellows and will understand."

FRIDAY 6th NOVEMBER 1908

The first cartoon featuring Charlton appeared in the *Kentish Independent* newspaper. The cartoons featured a Charlton fishmonger – the Addicker – called Arthur Bryant, who owned a fish shop in East Street. He was well known for supplying Charlton and their opponents with fish and chip meals after matches and gained further popularity when he started bringing a haddock fixed to a pole to Charlton games. Most cartoons in the *KI* featured Arthur and his fish and the first refers to a home match against the Royal Army Medical Corps in the Blackheath League which Charlton won 8-0.

SATURDAY 6th NOVEMBER 2004

Charlton exploited an unsettled Tottenham Hotspur side to record a fine 3-2 win at White Hart Lane. Spurs had been rocked by the resignation 24 hours earlier of Jacques Santini, with Martin Jol installed as caretaker. After 49 minutes, Charlton found themselves 3-0 up thanks to two goals from Shaun Bartlett and a deflected effort from Jerome Thomas. Bartlett was later sent off for handling on the line and Spurs fought back ferociously but Charlton clung on for a valuable three points.

SATURDAY 7th NOVEMBER 1964

Addicks boss Frank Hill was fuming after he claimed Charlton were robbed for the second year running at Cardiff. Charlton were convinced that Derek Tapscott's mis-hit 49th-minute shot did not cross the line. Addicks keeper Mike Rose said later: "My arm was between the ball and the line." Keith Ellis made it 2-0 before Eddie Firmani grabbed a 73rd-minute consolation. After the game, Hill stormed: "We lost a point here last season after John Charles handled the ball before scoring and now we've lost another because Cardiff got a goal they didn't even score!"

FRIDAY 8th NOVEMBER 1957

Llewellyn Charles 'Alan' Curbishley was born on this day in Forest Gate, east London, as one of five children born to a London docker and his wife. Curbishley attended Gainsborough Road Primary School, Trinity College School, Forest Gate and then West Ham Technical School. At 16, Curbishley joined West Ham United as an apprentice, making 87 full appearances for the Hammers before moving on to Birmingham City, Aston Villa, Charlton, Brighton & Hove Albion and back to Charlton, where he was made joint manager with Steve Gritt in July 1991.

SUNDAY 8th NOVEMBER 2009

A shocking display by Charlton saw a first-round FA Cup exit at the hands of non-league Northwich Victoria. Eighteen-year-old Wayne Riley struck nine minutes from time to spark jubilation among the home players and supporters. It was no more than Northwich deserved as they outfought Phil Parkinson's men in every department. It was the first time Charlton had lost to a non-league club since joining the Football League in 1921.

TUESDAY 9th NOVEMBER 1993

Charlton travelled to the eastern Italian coast to play Ancona in the Anglo-Italian Cup and returned with a 1-1 draw thanks to a Carl Leaburn goal after 60 minutes. Four weeks earlier, Charlton had lost 2-0 in Brescia and went on to lose two more home games in the competition against Ascoli and Pisa, both by three goals to nil.

SATURDAY 10th NOVEMBER 2007

Charlton climbed to second in the Championship with a comfortable 3-0 win over Cardiff City at The Valley. Sam Sodje and Chris Iwelumo both struck in first-half stoppage time and a straightforward victory was confirmed 10 minutes from time when Zheng Zhi headed home.

SATURDAY 11th NOVEMBER 2000

There was great fanfare when Charlton signed Iranian international Karim Bagheri for an initial fee of £400,000. Bagheri had been a star of Iran's 1998 World Cup campaign and, notably, had scored seven times in one qualifying game. But Bagheri appeared for just 17 minutes in a Charlton shirt, replacing Matt Svensson in a rain-drenched match at Ipswich on this day which Charlton lost 2-0.

FRIDAY 12th NOVEMBER 1999

Heavy motorway traffic made the already torturous journey to Grimsby even more difficult and four coachloads of Charlton supporters got delayed. They finally arrived at Blundell Park an hour late with the score two apiece. Whether their arrival inspired Charlton or not is hard to say, but the Addicks gave them something to smile about with three goals in 13 minutes to secure a 5-2 win. The victory moved Charlton to within a point of league leaders Manchester City, and manager Alan Curbishley admitted that expectations at the club were high.

SATURDAY 13th NOVEMBER 1982

All the talk was finally over as former European Footballer of the Year Allan Simonsen made his debut against Middlesbrough. If the aim was to generate added interest in Charlton, then Simonsen's arrival was a success: "The telephone hasn't stopped ringing since Allan joined us," said secretary Graham Hortop. "The demand for match tickets is so great we are opening our office at 10 in the morning." Almost 11,000 fans saw Charlton lose 3-2, but Simonsen grabbed a debut goal, generously credited to him despite a huge deflection.

SATURDAY 14th NOVEMBER 1959

Charlton boss Jimmy Trotter said a 'brick wall' would not have stopped Aston Villa after the Addicks crashed to a record-breaking 11-1 defeat. Goalkeeper Willie Duff conceded six before dislocating a finger. He was replaced by Don Townsend, who let in three before in turn giving way to Stuart Leary, who was beaten on two more occasions. Five of Villa's goals were scored by centre-forward Gerry Hitchens. After the game Trotter commented: "The team were like a ship in a storm without a captain."

TUESDAY 14th NOVEMBER 2006

Amid talk of player unrest, Charlton sacked head coach Iain Dowie and appointed assistant coach Les Reed in his place. Dowie was in charge for just five months and 15 games but in that time the club had fallen to the bottom of the Premiership and not won away. Chairman Richard Murray said the board thought long and hard before making the shock decision and said: "We had to consider whether we believed our current situation would improve and, reluctantly, we came to the conclusion that it would not."

WEDNESDAY 15th NOVEMBER 1967

When Lenny Glover left Charlton for Leicester City for £80,000 it was the highest fee ever paid for a winger. Kennington-born Glover made 196 appearances for Charlton, scoring 24 goals and winning admiration at The Valley for his trickery and crossing ability. Manager Eddie Firmani said: "I would have loved him to have stayed but he has consistently said he wants First Division football."

SATURDAY 16th NOVEMBER 1968

Charlton appeared on BBC's *Match of the Day* for the first time and, according to *Daily Express* reporter Norman Dixon, played some of the best football he had seen all season. Following a 1-1 draw, Dixon praised Addicks' midfielder Alan Campbell, saying he was 'invariably behind Charlton's fluid, imaginative, attacking moves.' Boss Eddie Firmani added: "We are creating chances and soon our luck in front of goal must change."

SATURDAY 17th NOVEMBER 1984

Daily Express reporter Don Woodward waxed lyrical after a highly-entertaining game at The Valley ended with Charlton's first victory over Birmingham City for 16 years. Woodward praised both teams for their enterprising play and said: "Give us more matches like this." Charlton won 2-1 thanks to goals from Mark Aizlewood and Robert Lee. Boss Lennie Lawrence said: "What a morale booster. Our first win in ten games, just as we go into a string of tough matches." His opposite number, former Addick Ron Saunders, responded in his usual droll fashion: "Three new players not match fit…Daley injured, Harford operation, Broadhurst and Hopkins ligaments, me broken heart."

SATURDAY 18th NOVEMBER 1978

Charlton boss Andy Nelson opted to single out big central defender Dave Shipperley for criticism after an extraordinary 5-5 draw at Bristol Rovers. The highest-scoring draw in the Football League for 12 years was a crazy, topsy-turvy affair in which nine goals were scored in a mad 38 minutes. But Nelson said: "Shipperley was involved in every goal we conceded. The score was more like Shipperley 5 Charlton 5." 'Big Ship' as he was affectionately known by Charlton fans was hard done by. It was one of those games which defied logic. Mike Flanagan and Martin Robinson both scored twice for Charlton following Dick Tydeman's 14th-minute opener.

MONDAY 19th NOVEMBER 2001

Charlton emerged with a point from a pulsating, goal-ridden London
derby against West Ham United thanks to a last gasp leveller from Jonatan
Johansson. A superb, breathless game, shown live on Sky TV, ended 4-4
and became the highest scoring draw in a Premiership London derby. A
Paul Kitson hat-trick and a goal from Jermain Defoe were equalled by
doubles from Jason Euell and Johansson. It was the first time that Charlton
had scored as many as four goals in successive London derbies following
the amazing performance at Highbury on November 4th.

SATURDAY 20th NOVEMBER 1982

Talented Charlton defender Paul Elliott launched an extraordinary
attack on his team-mates after the Addicks were humiliated 5-1 at home
by Rotherham United. The outspoken 18-year-old said even the signing
of Allan Simonsen could not keep him at The Valley: "I no longer want
to play in a team with four or five cheats and that's what we have here,"
said Elliott. "Several players were not trying on this day. I can make up
for one player not trying, but not half a team." After the game Elliott had
been sought out by Rotherham player-manager Emlyn Hughes, who
encouraged him to stay focused and seek out a bigger club.

TUESDAY 21st NOVEMBER 1961

Former Scottish international wing-half Frank 'Tiger' Hill, aged 55,
was appointed Charlton's new manager following the sacking of Jimmy
Trotter. Hill, who as a player won three league championship medals
with Arsenal, had previously managed Crewe Alexandra, Burnley,
Preston North End and Notts County.

MONDAY 22nd NOVEMBER 1982

The night of the Rotherham United debacle, Charlton chairman Mark
Hulyer told manager Ken Craggs over dinner that his job was safe.
Forty hours later Craggs was sacked. Craggs said: "That was hard to
take. It hurt. But I bear no malice against Hulyer. Given time I would
have put things right at Charlton, of that I am certain. I was not against
the signing of Allan Simonsen but it dragged on for so long that it
made you wonder if it was right or wrong." Former Bolton Wanderers
and Wolverhampton Wanderers manager Ian Greaves was an early
contender to take Craggs's place.

SATURDAY 22nd NOVEMBER 2008

After a run of eight games without a win, culminating in today's humiliating 5-2 defeat to Sheffield United at The Valley, Charlton sacked manager Alan Pardew. Pardew arrived at Charlton in December 2006 following the disastrous brief tenure of Les Reed. Despite almost saving Charlton from relegation from the Premiership, the team started struggling in the Championship. Pardew said: "My record coming to this club has been good but it's been difficult here. When I arrived they were on the slide and I haven't been able to stop that."

SATURDAY 23rd NOVEMBER 1974

Fighting on the terraces marred this FA Cup first-round tie against Southern League side Chelmsford City. A crowd of 6,058 crammed into 'The Stadium', home of the Essex club, and saw a single goal from Arthur Horsfield after 37 minutes give Charlton a 1-0 victory. Defender Harry Cripps was unimpressed with the challenge Chelmsford posed: "I expected it to be much tougher," he said.

TUESDAY 24th NOVEMBER 1981

Four goals were scored in seven crazy minutes at The Valley as Charlton lost by the odd goal in seven to London neighbours Chelsea. Just two minutes were on the clock when Clive Walker beat Nicky Johns to make it 1-0 to the visitors. Things went positively mad after 28 minutes when Martin Robinson equalised for the Addicks. Three minutes later Derek Hales put Charlton ahead. Two minutes after that Walker got his second to make it 2-2 and then two minutes later, future Addick John Bumstead made it 3-2. Bumstead got a second on 54 before Leroy Ambrose got his first goal in a Charlton shirt after 80 minutes to make the final score Charlton 3 Chelsea 4.

TUESDAY 25th NOVEMBER 1986

So where were the missing four? That was the joke doing the rounds after just 817 fans turned up to watch this evening's Full Members' Cup third-round tie at Selhurst Park against Bradford City. The attendance was four less than the 821 that had watched Charlton beat Birmingham City in the previous round. The four absentees missed Charlton score twice in two minutes through Robert Lee and Colin Walsh to win 2-0.

SATURDAY 26th NOVEMBER 1932

Despite a superb hat-trick by Charlton's prolific striker Cyril Pearce, the Addicks were on the end of a 7-3 thrashing at West Ham United, with the Hammers scoring three times in the opening eight minutes. The best player on the pitch, according to the press, was West Ham's right-winger Tommy Yews, although Pearce's hat-trick 'surpassed everything for individual brilliance'.

SATURDAY 27th NOVEMBER 1982

Ian Greaves, David Pleat and John Hollins were, in turn, installed as favourites to land the vacant manager's job at Charlton. All the time, a low-profile 34-year-old named Lennie Lawrence was managing in a caretaker capacity and he took charge for the first time when the side travelled to Shrewsbury Town and got a 0-0 draw.

SATURDAY 28th NOVEMBER 1970

Charlton manager Theo Foley said his players were so excited at being 3-0 up at half-time at Queens Park Rangers that he had to calm them down. Perhaps the players could be forgiven though. Charlton had not won away from home since the 15th of March 1969, a run of 35 matches. Two goals from Ray Treacy and Mike Kenning eventually gave the Addicks a 4-1 victory.

SATURDAY 29th NOVEMBER 1969

At the time of his death aged 70, Seth Plum was working as a petrol pump attendant in his home community of Tottenham, north London. Born in 1899, he died on this day in St Ann's Hospital, but earns his place in Charlton's history as the club's first player to win a full international cap.

SATURDAY 30th NOVEMBER 1968

"What a grand game!" enthused chairman Michael Gliksten after Charlton beat Fulham 5-3 at The Valley. Alan Campbell and Harry Gregory, who scored twice, were the chief architects of Charlton's victory in which, according to reporter Marshall Fallows, both sides adopted 'refreshing, all-out attacking methods'. Charlton's other goals were scored by Dennis Booth (2) and Graham Moore. The win kept Charlton two points behind Second Division leaders Derby County and manager Eddie Firmani said: "Let's hope we can keep it up. We are in a very handy position."

CHARLTON ATHLETIC
On This Day

DECEMBER

SATURDAY 1st DECEMBER 1934

When Henry 'Harry' Wright injured his back at Northampton Town it opened the door for Sam Bartram, who made his Charlton debut on this day at Watford and played his first match at The Valley the following Saturday against Newport County. Though Wright was back between the sticks for a 6-3 win at Gillingham, it would not be long before Bartram claimed the position for his own. By the third game of the 1935/36 season, Bartram had established himself. He would not be shifted for more than 20 years.

SATURDAY 1st DECEMBER 1979

Back in the 1970s, foreign transfers made headline news and, when Charlton included newly-signed Danes Viggo Lund Jacobsen and Johnny Ostergaard in the squad to face West Ham United, there was huge interest. Charlton marked the occasion in a manner which, in hindsight, looks a little extravagant. Members of the Danish embassy were invited, Danish and British flags were hung from the floodlight pylons and the match was beamed back live to Denmark. It appeared to inspire bottom-of-the-table Charlton, who beat the Hammers for the first time in 43 years thanks to a 15th-minute goal from Steve Gritt.

SATURDAY 2nd DECEMBER 2006

Boss Les Reed said he was 'devastated' after Charlton lost a vital Premiership six-pointer against Sheffield United at Bramall Lane. Despite leading for much of the game thanks to an Andy Reid effort, Charlton could not hang on and were finally undone by goals from Chris Morgan and a volley from Keith Gillespie. The result was a disaster for Charlton and manager Reed could not hide his disappointment.

WEDNESDAY 3rd DECEMBER 1975

Andy Nelson said Charlton were 'in the muck' after a 5-1 home defeat to troubled Luton Town, their worst at The Valley for five years. The debt-ridden Hatters brushed Charlton aside, prompting Addicks boss Nelson, whose father died on the morning of the match, to say: "We are deep in it but it is nice to know early that you are in trouble." A Mike Flanagan goal gave the Addicks the lead on eight minutes but that was the only note of optimism during Charlton's first home floodlit defeat since April 1972.

SATURDAY 4th DECEMBER 1982

To get some idea of the stature of Charlton's astonishing capture of Allan Simonsen, consider this: an estimated 60 per cent of Denmark's four million inhabitants watched live television coverage of today's match at The Valley against Newcastle United. And the Dane didn't disappoint, scoring Charlton's second in a comfortable 2-0 victory. Among the 10,371 spectators was Cardinal Basil Hume, a Newcastle fan, who was very impressed with Simonsen's performance: "He had some lovely touches," said the cardinal. "His goal was an absolute beauty."

SATURDAY 5th DECEMBER 1992

A truly momentous and happy day for Charlton Athletic which only seems to improve with the passage of time. After a miserable, seven-year exile dominated by political wrangling, red tape and several false dawns, the football club returned to its beloved Valley ground, a triumph of hope over adversity. Everything about the day was perfect. There was a carnival atmosphere in and around the ground and an overwhelming sense of relief and justice. From the moment chairman Roger Alwen symbolically unlocked the main gates at noon to let the first fans in, to the parading of former Valley legends such as 'Sailor' Brown and Derek Hales and, of course, Colin Walsh's seventh-minute winner, everything was just how Charlton fans had hoped it would be. Almost two decades on, the occasion has a dream-like quality. Indeed, for Charlton fans, 5th December 1992 was quite simply proof that, sometimes, dreams really do come true.

TUESDAY 5th DECEMBER 1995

On the third anniversary of the glorious return to The Valley, Charlton travelled to neighbours and rivals Millwall and emerged with a memorable 2-0 win. In an incident-packed game, played in driving snow with the obligatory orange ball, both sides were reduced to ten men. Lee Bowyer was sent off after 21 minutes and, on 57, Millwall skipper Keith Stevens got his marching orders. Two goals from Kim Grant, one in each half, completed a great victory for the Addicks in a game also remembered for a remarkable cameo role by Paul Mortimer who, after replacing David Whyte after 49 minutes, was simply outstanding and demonstrated skills rarely seen at this level of the game.

SUNDAY 5th DECEMBER 2004

Goalkeeper Dean Kiely and Danish winger Dennis Rommedahl were the heroes as Charlton snatched a last gasp winner at arch rivals Crystal Palace. Kiely saved Andy Johnson's spot-kick and then, in the dying seconds of injury time, Rommedahl struck an unstoppable winner. Delighted boss Alan Curbishley said: "He showed within an instant what he is about." Rommedahl added: "The goal and the win mean a lot to me and the rest of the lads."

SATURDAY 6th DECEMBER 1958

During yet another thriller at The Valley, the irrepressible Stuart Leary scored his 100th league goal for Charlton. Bristol Rovers were the visitors for this Second Division clash, watched by 13,789. A breathless first half ended with Charlton 3-2 up and Leary, who had scored two, a goal-scoring centurion. Rovers equalised but Sam Lawrie kept his head and scored from the penalty spot – also his second goal – to clinch the points for the Addicks.

WEDNESDAY 7th DECEMBER 1988

"I can't tell you what this means to our club," said a delighted Peter Shirtliff after Charlton became the six-a-side soccer champions. The Addicks picked up a £51,000 prize for winning the Guinness Soccer Six Championship at Manchester's G-Mex centre. They did it in style, scoring 22 goals in their six games and notching up impressive 6-3 and 6-2 wins against Liverpool and West Ham United in the final stages. In the final itself they beat Nottingham Forest 2-1. Charlton boss Lennie Lawrence said: "It's a long time since there was any silverware in our cabinet and let's hope this is the start of something to look forward to."

SATURDAY 8th DECEMBER 2001

What was it about striker Kevin Lisbie and borrowed boots? Three days before this day's impressive 3-1 win over Tottenham Hotspur, Lisbie had grabbed an 89th-minute winner at Stamford Bridge, wearing someone else's boots after his own were stolen. Lisbie had also grabbed a spectacular late winner against Ipswich Town at Portman Road in August, again wearing someone else's footwear. He still hadn't sorted out his own pair by the time the Spurs game came around but still managed to score twice to earn a valuable three points.

SATURDAY 9th DECEMBER 2000

In what is surely the greatest game played at The Valley to date since the 1992 homecoming, Charlton held all-conquering Manchester United to a 3-3 draw in a quite incredible match. The Addicks tore into Alex Ferguson's side from the off and came close on a couple of occasions before getting their reward after 10 minutes through Shaun Bartlett. United, inspired by the brilliant Ryan Giggs, then raced into a 3-1 lead with goals from Giggs, Solskjaer and Keane. But Charlton stormed back and a second goal from Bartlett on 79 minutes and then a dramatic late equaliser from John Robinson gave them a share of the spoils and left The Valley rocking. After the game boss Alan Curbishley said: "It was a cracking match and great entertainment for those fortunate enough to be here."

SATURDAY 10th DECEMBER 1983

An 87th-minute goal by Woolwich-born defender Paul Curtis gave Charlton a hard-earned victory at Fulham. It was the Addicks' first away win in 23 attempts since a 2-1 win at Leeds United in November 1982, and manager Lennie Lawrence described it as the best performance away from The Valley that he could remember.

SATURDAY 11th DECEMBER 1948

Season 1948/49 saw a dramatic increase in attendances, and the number of people watching Charlton home and away was a staggering 1,603,781, including 844,537 at The Valley. On this day, Charlton edged a seven-goal thriller against Arsenal watched by 51,517 fans. On five occasions, attendances at The Valley topped the 50,000 mark, with the biggest of all being 61,475 against champions-elect Portsmouth on January 22nd 1949. It meant that Charlton's average gate was 40,216 – the highest ever.

SUNDAY 11th DECEMBER 2005

More than 600 people attended Charlton's official centenary dinner at the Royal Lancaster Hotel in London. Those who attended saw a specially produced 11-minute film of the club's history. There was an upbeat mood at the dinner as, the previous day, the team had ended a run of five consecutive Premiership defeats by beating Sunderland 2-0 with goals from two Darrens – Bent and Ambrose.

SUNDAY 12th DECEMBER 1976

Derek Hales was in typically confident mood after signing for Derby County for £333,333. Described in the papers as 'the most wanted striker in the country'. Hales told reporters: "I intend to score the goals Derby have bought me to get. My make-up thrives on goals and I'll always back myself to get between 20 and 30 goals a season. I don't think it will be any harder to score in the First Division than the Second." Derby fought off rival bids from West Ham United and Anderlecht to secure Hales's services.

SUNDAY 13th DECEMBER 1987

A highly controversial late goal gave Charlton their first win at Tottenham Hotspur in 32 years and sent several thousands Addicks fans wild with delight. A Sunday morning kick-off at White Hart Lane was goalless with seven minutes remaining when Charlton striker Paul Williams and Spurs keeper Tony Parks contested a 50-50 ball. The pair collided, the ball broke and David Campbell had the simple task of slotting the ball home. Parks was left with two cracked teeth and a cut tongue. The decision by referee Ray Lewis to allow the goal infuriated Spurs boss Terry Venables, who said: "I blame the referee. Goalkeepers are supposed to be protected." But Charlton boss Lennie Lawrence hit back, saying: "There's not an ounce of malice in Paul Williams and I don't think it was a foul."

SUNDAY 14th DECEMBER 1947

How appropriate that Lennie Lawrence – a man destined to become inextricably associated with the trials and tribulations of Charlton during the 1980s – should be born in the year that Charlton won the cup. Lennie never played professional football, though while working as a PE teacher he did play at amateur level for Croydon, Carshalton Athletic and Sutton United. Before joining Charlton as a reserve team coach, Lennie worked under Malcolm Allison at Plymouth Argyle. Lawrence assumed the helm after the brief stewardship of Ken Craggs and proved to be an inspired appointment by otherwise vilified chairman Mark Hulyer. Lawrence later went on to manage Middlesbrough, Bradford City, Luton Town, Grimsby Town and Cardiff City, was director of football at Bristol Rovers and Hereford and assistant manager at Crystal Palace.

THURSDAY 15th DECEMBER 1983

The aforementioned Lawrence was always good value to express real opinions rather than banal platitudes to the press and, after Charlton beat Leeds United 2-0 at The Valley tonight, he bemoaned the fact that no-one was helping the club escape from its perilous financial plight: "I find it amazing and totally frustrating," he said. "The team is doing better than it has done for years but still no-one is coming in to help us. Our results have established a platform on which we could build if the club were re-financed." Leeds manager Eddie Gray agreed: "Charlton are a different team from the one we played last year. Full credit must go to everyone at the club for the way they are playing."

SATURDAY 16th DECEMBER 1905

The first recorded game of Charlton Athletic Football Club took place on this day at Siemen's Meadow, an area of rough ground virtually on the banks of the River Thames, next to the Royal Dockyard at Woolwich. The friendly match was played against a team based just north of the Thames called Silvertown Wesley United. Charlton won the game 6-1 and a report in the *Kentish Independent* the following Friday read: "Silvertown Wesley met with yet another reverse on Saturday last, being defeated by Charlton Athletic at Charlton. Wesley were outclassed in every department with the exception of Kersley, the goalkeeper, who played a magnificent match throughout."

FRIDAY 16th DECEMBER 1932

Sandy MacFarlane returned for a second stint as Charlton manager in June 1928 and enjoyed quick success. He did superbly well to win Division Three South in his first year despite the club being in deep financial trouble, and then consolidated their position in Division Two for three seasons. But the club started season 1932/33 disastrously and, with relegation staring the club in the face, the board decided MacFarlane had to go. Following a private meeting in Stratford, director David Clark was despatched to pass on the news to MacFarlane, who received £1,000. For the second time, Albert Lindon stepped in to take the reins. Lindon managed the side until May 1933, when Jimmy Seed arrived. Lindon remained as assistant manager until the termination of his employment in May 1934.

SATURDAY 17th DECEMBER 1938

Everton's Goodison Park was a fortress in season 1938/39, but Jimmy Seed's Charlton shattered their unbeaten record and won 4-1 on a mudbath. According to a *Daily Express* reporter: "They (Everton) were given a football lesson by Charlton, who banged the ball about with the knowledge that it was the only way to reach goal through the slush." Goals from 'Monty' Wilkinson, 'Sailor' Brown and a brace from George Tadman earned Charlton an impressive victory.

FRIDAY 18th DECEMBER 2009

Charlton and Millwall announced they were dedicating the following day's derby match at The Valley to the memories of Rob Knox and Jimmy Mizen. The teenagers were supporters of the respective clubs and were both murdered in separate incidents in 2008. Both clubs used the game to spread a hard-hitting message aimed at eradicating knife crime. The sponsors' names on team shirts were replaced with the 'Street Violence Ruins Lives' campaign logo. The game proved to be a 4-4 classic and a worthy tribute to the memories of Rob and Jimmy.

TUESDAY 19th DECEMBER 2006

Head coach Les Reed was clinging to his job by a thread after Charlton's season plummeted to new depths with a home defeat to Wycombe Wanderers in the quarter-finals of the Carling Cup. A thoroughly inept performance by Charlton saw the Chairboys leave SE7 with a 1-0 victory which would have been greater had it not been for the efforts of Addicks keeper Scott Carson. The players left the field to cries of 'you're not fit to wear the shirt' from angry and deflated fans.

SATURDAY 20th DECEMBER 1980

Charlton boss Mike Bailey paid tribute to his troops after a 2-1 victory at The Valley over Carlisle United extended their record-breaking unbeaten league and cup run to 17 games. "They battled for me," said Bailey. "They gave everything they've got." Despite Owen Brown giving the Cumbrians the lead on 14, second-half goals from Colin Powell and an own goal by Ian Macdonald ensured the brilliant run continued. Man of the Match, however, was a diminutive, nimble playmaker called Peter Beardsley, who shone for Carlisle.

CHARLTON'S SEASON PLUMMETED TO NEW DEPTHS IN DECEMBER 2006, WITH A HOME DEFEAT TO WYCOMBE WANDERERS IN THE QUARTER-FINALS OF THE CARLING CUP

SATURDAY 21st DECEMBER 1957

A momentous, logic-defying match that could quite justifiably lay claim to being the greatest and most dramatic in English Football League history. With just 28 minutes left to play, 10-man Charlton trailed 5-1 at The Valley to Bill Shankly's Huddersfield Town. Apparently granted magical powers after changing his boots at half-time, Addicks striker Johnny Summers proceeded to rewrite the record books with an astonishing performance which had the Charlton fans gasping for breath. He had already grabbed Charlton's first goal on 47 minutes but then, unbelievably, went on to score four more in 17 minutes, all with his 'wrong' right foot. 'Buck' Ryan had added another for the Addicks and, with four minutes left, Town equalised to make it 6-6. That had to be that but, with The Valley crowd shouting themselves hoarse with excitement, Summers put Ryan clear with one minute left and he shot past Sandy Kennon to give the depleted Addicks a quite extraordinary victory. The next day's papers struggled to find the right words to describe a game that would have seemed far-fetched in a comic. "The most amazing match in football," screamed the *News of the World*, and "ten men make soccer history – last seconds goal wins a fantastic match," said the *Sunday Express*. Quite simply, those Charlton fans who witnessed it will never forget it.

SATURDAY 22nd DECEMBER 1923

Charlton played their first match at The Mount in Catford in front of 6,000 fans against Northampton Town. Monday's Daily Express reported: "Circumstances prevented the occasion being a complete success. The weather was almost as bad as it could possibly be, and only the most enthusiastic of the club's supporters were present." Those that did venture to Catford witnessed a dull game which ended goalless.

SATURDAY 23rd DECEMBER 2000

Alan Curbishley was a relieved man after Charlton ground out a priceless win at The Valley against Walter Smith's Everton. An eighth-minute goal from Matt Svensson, who headed past Thomas Myhre from a corner, was enough to claim all three points. After Charlton's first win in five games, Curbishley told reporters: "I was hoping for a win and I didn't care how we got it. I didn't mind if it came from a shocking performance as long as we got three points."

SUNDAY 24th DECEMBER 2006

Alan Pardew was appointed Charlton's new manager after head coach Les Reed left the club by mutual consent. After Saturday's 2-0 reverse at Middlesbrough, Charlton were seven points adrift of Premiership safety. The appointment was made public at 7pm on Christmas Eve and chairman Richard Murray said: "We are very fortunate a manager of Alan Pardew's calibre is available and we have moved very, very quickly to secure his services."

SATURDAY 25th DECEMBER 1937

The fog was so bad during Charlton's match against Chelsea at Stamford Bridge that the game was abandoned after 61 minutes with the score at 1-1. Except nobody told Charlton keeper Sam Bartram! Twenty-one players returned to the dressing room, leaving a solitary ginger-haired goalkeeper out on the pitch. Bartram obviously thought his side had Chelsea pinned in their own half and assumed the game was continuing. It was not until a policeman found the great man ten minutes later that he realised that the match was over. Much hilarity and merciless ribbing among his team-mates ensued.

TUESDAY 26th DECEMBER 1967

A brilliant fightback saw Charlton score three times in the last 25 minutes to clinch an unlikely draw against Norwich at The Valley. The Canaries were two up inside 11 minutes and added a third just after half-time. Charlton then woke up – first, ex-Canary Gordon Bolland scrambled the ball over the line, and then a shot from Graham Moore went in off a post. In an incredible finale, Harry Gregory squeezed the ball past City keeper Kevin Keelan to salvage a point for the Addicks.

SUNDAY 26th DECEMBER 1999

Charlton's 2-1 victory over Crystal Palace at The Valley was the start of an astonishing run which saw them record 12 successive league victories. Goals from John Salako and Swede Martin Pringle clinched the win. After the game, boss Alan Curbishley said Pringle needed to show more fire: "He needs to know what his attributes are, like his pace," said Curbs. "And he needs to be more aggressive in his game."

FRIDAY 26th DECEMBER 2003

A brilliant Boxing Day performance by Charlton saw moneybags Chelsea blown away 4-2 at The Valley. Masterful performances by Scott Parker and Paolo Di Canio were the inspiration behind a display which had the Charlton fans drooling. Goals from Hermann Hreidarsson, Matt Holland, Jonatan Johansson and Jason Euell proved decisive. After the game, boss Alan Curbishley said: "We have got the confidence we want to go looking for a European spot."

SATURDAY 26th DECEMBER 2009

Wild scenes of celebration engulfed The Valley after an extraordinary comeback by nine-man Charlton against Swindon Town. Sam Sodje and Deon Burton both received their marching orders in the first half, but Charlton still edged ahead courtesy of a fine strike by Jonjo Shelvey. Town made their two-man advantage count in the second half and, as the game entered its final minute, led 2-1. With seconds remaining, a long ball from Jose Semedo reached Miguel Llera, who finished superbly with a sublime lob to spark celebration among the Charlton fans.

TUESDAY 27th DECEMBER 1960

How often does a game of professional football end 6-4? What then, are the chances of two teams playing each other twice in 24 hours and both games finishing with that result? That, though, is what happened when Charlton and Plymouth Argyle locked horns in 1960. On Boxing Day at The Valley, goals from Stuart Leary, Don Townsend and two each for Johnny Summers and Dennis Edwards gave Charlton the win. The teams then travelled to Devon and, 24 hours later at Home Park, astonishingly, The Pilgrims won by the same score, with Wilf Carter becoming the only Argyle player ever to score five times in a league match.

SATURDAY 27th DECEMBER 1975

Opposing managers Eddie McCreadie and Andy Nelson had very different perspectives after Charlton grabbed a shock 3-2 win at Chelsea. McCreadie said: "We have some exceptional footballers and make other sides look like carthorses but we still don't win." But Nelson dismissed McCreadie's view saying: "Anybody can play it across the park. But the game is all about getting the ball in the net." A goal from left-back Phil Warman and a brace from Derek Hales secured the points for Charlton.

TUESDAY 28th DECEMBER 1965

Goalkeeper Les Surman made a nightmare start in his only appearance for Charlton, conceding after 18 seconds. In freezing conditions at Portsmouth, Surman stood rooted to the spot as a suicidal back header from Billy Bonds trickled past him. Charlton lost the game 3-1. Surman never played for Charlton again and died at the tragically young age of 31.

SUNDAY 28th DECEMBER 1986

Under-pressure Charlton turned on the style and climbed off the bottom of the old First Division with a fine 5-0 win over Manchester City at Selhurst Park. Colin Walsh was the architect of the rout, plundering two superb goals with his cultured left foot. Charlton played superbly and manager Lennie Lawrence purred: "I could not be more pleased because this was our most important match since the one in which we gained promotion last season."

MONDAY 28th DECEMBER 1998

Arsenal boss Arsène Wenger branded Charlton midfielder Neil Redfearn 'a cheat' after Gunners midfielder Patrick Vieira was sent off by referee Uriah Rennie 51 minutes into a controversial clash at The Valley. Despite the Frenchman blatantly elbowing Redfearn right in front of Rennie's gaze, Wenger claimed Redfearn went down too easily. It prompted a war-of-words between the two clubs, with Alan Curbishley calling a press conference in which he blasted Wenger for his allegations against Redfearn. Despite the FA refusing to overturn Rennie's decision, Wenger persisted, pointing out that more fouls had been awarded against Redfearn than any other player in the Premiership and slamming Eddie Youds for a tackle on Dennis Bergkamp in the same match, which Arsenal won 1-0.

SATURDAY 29th DECEMBER 1990

A superb game against Ipswich Town at Portman Road ended 4-4, with Charlton twice clawing back a two-goal deficit. Goals from Andy Peake and Paul Mortimer made it 2-2 after Town had led 2-0 through goals from Stockwell and Thompson. The Suffolk side then restored their two-goal advantage before Alex Dyer made it 4-3. With four minutes remaining, Charlton were awarded a penalty. Up stepped Tommy Caton to smash the ball past Craig Forrest, sending the Charlton following behind the goal wild with delight.

SATURDAY 30th DECEMBER 2000

Charlton were humiliated at West Ham United on Boxing Day, losing 5-0 in a game which Alan Curbishley described as 'an embarrassment'. The squad that travelled north to Manchester City on this day were under pressure to restore some pride into the shirt, and they did just that with a fine performance which ended in a 4-1 win. Two goals from Jonatan Johansson, a penalty from Graham Stuart and a fourth from Claus Jensen blew City away. Jensen's goal was extraordinary – a clearance by Richard Dunne struck Jensen's legs with such force that it travelled 40 yards and sailed over the head of stranded City keeper Nicky Weaver and into the net. Alan Curbishley said: "It was a fantastic response to the West Ham game."

WEDNESDAY 31st DECEMBER 2008

Charlton caretaker boss Phil Parkinson was appointed manager on a full-time basis, six weeks after the sacking of Alan Pardew. With the Addicks rooted to the bottom of the Championship, Parkinson's first job was to try and ensure survival. Chairman Richard Murray said: "The overwhelming feeling was that Phil was the best man to lead us and rescue us from our current plight." Forty-one-year-old Parkinson said: "I'm obviously delighted with the board's decision and I fully intend to make the most of this opportunity."

FRIDAY 31st DECEMBER 2010

After weeks of speculation, a new company called CAFC Holdings Limited (CAFCH) took over Charlton. CAFCH owner and controller Michael Slater became the new club chairman, replacing Richard Murray, who remained as a director. Slater said: "As the new owners, we are both football fans and businessmen. Today's acquisition brings much-needed financial stability to the club." It gave Charlton fans everywhere a reason to celebrate and hope for a more successful future.